Biblical Fundamentalism

What Every Catholic Should Know

Ronald D. Witherup, S.S.

THE LITURGICAL PRESS
Collegeville, Minnesota

www.litpress.org

Cover design by David Manahan, O.S.B. Photo courtesy of PHOTODISC.

Nihil Obstat: Rev. Paul P. Zilonka, C.P.
Imprimatur: Most Rev. W. Francis Malooly, Auxiliary Bishop of Baltimore, January 25, 2001.

3   4   5   6   7   8

Library of Congress Cataloging-in-Publication Data

Witherup, Ronald D., 1950–
    Biblical fundamentalism : what every Catholic should know / Ronald D. Witherup.
        p. cm.
    Includes bibliographical references.
    ISBN 0-8146-2722-6 (alk. paper)
    1. Fundamentalism. 2. Catholic Church—Apologetic works. I. Title.

BT82.2 .W58 2001
220'.088'22–dc21

                                                    2001029259

In grateful memory of

Dr. A. Vanlier Hunter, Jr.
1939–1992

Contents

Preface

As we move into the third Christian millennium, it is surprising to see how many issues in religious discourse continue to provoke disagreement among Christians about certain basic elements of faith. This is the case of the Bible. How to read and interpret the Bible remains a vital Christian question.

Sociological data has shown that biblical fundamentalism has made inroads among Catholics in recent years. For some Catholics who are hungry to have the Bible become a more central element of their faith and in their daily lives, there is no perceived problem with a fundamentalist approach. For others, the issues that are often raised during encounters with fundamentalists provoke a host of questions and a basic insecurity about their own Catholic identity.

In speaking engagements with Catholics around the country in the last fifteen years, I have been asked to address many issues over and over again that grow out of the phenomenon of biblical fundamentalism. This book is the result of those encounters. I trust that it will be a useful handbook for Catholics who are both intrigued by and perhaps worried about the questions that arise when they desire to use "the good book" in their personal lives. It may also help Protestants who want to understand better a Roman Catholic approach to the Bible.

I am grateful to all my former students and audiences who have helped shape my response to fundamentalism. I also thank the many scholars whose work has informed my own and who, because of the nature of this popular text, cannot be duly acknowledged. I dedicate this book to the memory of one of my first professors of Bible, Dr. A. Vanlier Hunter, Jr., who was an inspiration to a generation of Catholic seminarians at St. Mary's Seminary and University in Baltimore. Van, as he was affectionately known, died prematurely of cancer after nearly twenty years as a Presbyterian minister and biblical scholar sojourning in a Roman Catholic seminary. His Reformed tradition background, with its strong commitment to the Word of God, served him well in the setting, both as a professor of sacred Scripture and as associate dean of the school's Ecumenical Institute. He was ever the grassroots ecumenist. From him I learned a great deal about tolerance and dialogue, but I also learned how to make the Bible come alive in preaching and in the classroom. I thank him posthumously for his zeal, his dedication, and his gentle teaching.

I also thank Professor Paul Zilonka, C.P., for his generous reading of the manuscript and helpful suggestions, and Dr. Cecil White, the Baptist librarian of St. Patrick Seminary in Menlo Park, California, for many helpful conversations and professional assistance. While I believe their contributions helped to improve the book, any shortcomings are naturally my own. Finally, I owe a great debt of gratitude to Mark Twomey, Peter Dwyer, and the entire staff at The Liturgical Press for their enthusiasm for and encouragement of this project. Their support made the task of producing a concise manuscript much easier than it otherwise would have been.

R.D.W.
First Sunday of Advent, 2000

Introduction

When I was growing up in the 1950s, it was commonplace as a Catholic to contrast Catholicism with Protestantism in a rather simple way. Protestants had the Bible as their guide; Catholics had the sacraments. Catholics were, generally speaking, quite ignorant of the Bible. We relied upon the teachings of the Church as communicated mostly through Sunday sermons and catechism classes.

Vatican Council II (1962–1965) changed all that. Pope John XXIII's convocation of a world-wide ecumenical council threw open the windows of the Church to let in the fresh air of *aggiornamento*–thoroughgoing renewal. One of the most significant changes to be initiated by the council was the direct encouragement to Catholics to rediscover the Bible. Vatican II began a veritable revolution among Catholics in the way they viewed the Bible and how they used it in their lives. No longer relegated to the bookshelf, to the coffee table, or to the confines of a monastery, and no longer used mainly to record the sacramental events of Catholic life such as baptisms, weddings, and funerals, the Bible began to play a prominent role in Catholic life.

The liturgy itself reflected this dramatic change. The Church revised and updated the ancient tool of a lectionary, the official book of readings for the Church liturgical year, as part of its liturgical renewal. Now it contains a wide selection of readings from both the Old and New Testaments proclaimed at Mass over the span of a three-year liturgical cycle.

It introduced Catholics to passages they had never explored and seldom ever heard addressed from the pulpit. Catholics had their appetites whetted for more biblical nourishment and, fortunately, Catholic biblical scholars who had quietly been doing their work behind the scenes for decades began to publish and lecture widely on the Bible.

Bible study groups began to multiply, but many Catholic parishes could not keep pace with the desire of Catholics for more knowledge of the Bible. Many Catholics were attracted to non-Catholic Bible study groups, some of which were fundamentalist in their orientation, and sometimes vehemently anti-Catholic in their demeanor. Catholics often encountered biblical fundamentalism whether they recognized it or not.

Vatican II produced a two-sided reality when it fostered Catholic interest in the Bible. One side positively reinforced the truth that Catholics, too, are Christians who accept the Bible as God's holy Word which provides a moral compass for Christian living. Catholics were urged to get familiar with the Bible. It is our book, too. The other side, however, is that grassroots Catholic education about the Bible has lagged behind Catholic interest in exploring the Bible and its mysteries. In addition, some Evangelical Protestants have aggressively targeted disaffected Catholics to entice them toward their denomination and their way of reading the Bible. The result is that one's admirable interest in knowing more about the Bible is sometimes undermined by misguided instruction about it, especially from a fundamentalist perspective.

I should issue the reader a caution at this point. I have no desire to heap coals on a fire of sharp-tongued animosity between Bible-toting fundamentalist Evangelical Protestants and fearful, paranoid Catholics. Some people can oppose fundamentalism in a way that is both un-Christian and demeaning. They ridicule biblical fundamentalists as ignorant bigots who misuse the Bible for whatever suits them. There is no need for name-calling and vicious stereotyping, although such activity takes place occasionally on both sides of the fence. In my experience, fundamentalism can appear in multiple forms. We tend to categorize it as an ultra-conservative movement when in reality there are liberal forms of a type of fundamentalism that are just as unbending and uncompromising as those on the conservative right. But I am getting ahead of myself.

I attempt to address the question of how Catholicism should interact with fundamentalism in a fair-minded fashion. Yet I must also admit that I perceive a problem with fundamentalism. I have personally encountered it in my travels and speaking engagements in the U.S. and abroad. It is a serious issue that confronts Catholics on a daily basis. In some areas of Africa I have seen the impact of Seventh Day Adventist attacks on Catholic faith and the questions that it raises in the minds of those who have to live in such an environment. In Latin America and South America I have seen and have heard of the attempts of several Evangelical, fundamentalist groups to entice Catholics away from their faith. They point out Catholicism's alleged deficiencies as anti-biblical and non-Christian. In many parts of the U.S. itself, not simply in the Bible Belt, I have witnessed the influence of biblical fundamentalists and the doubts that their rhetoric raises in the minds of many Catholics.

In almost all the public lectures on the Bible I have given since the mid-1980s I have been asked over and over again by Catholics how they should respond to one question or another that has been asked of them by fundamentalist friends, relatives, or neighbors. These are questions like, "Father, what do I say when I am asked, 'Are you saved?'" or "How can I explain to my friends why we believe in the pope?" or "My friends say Catholics aren't going to heaven because they don't accept Jesus Christ as their personal Lord and Savior." At the very least, the language of fundamentalism is unfamiliar and often makes Catholics uncomfortable. Couple that with a basic insecurity about the contents of the Bible, and the stage is set for some self-questioning that can, and does, lead to real religious anxiety for some Catholics.

In my judgment there is a pastoral urgency to the question of how Catholics think about the Bible. Many Catholics whom I meet do not feel comfortable with their knowledge about the Bible, especially in light of what some of their Protestant friends say. Biblical literacy is not our strong suit.

(Then again, my Protestant colleagues tell me that the average Protestant is not as knowledgeable about the Bible as we might suppose.) The fact is that contemporary American culture exposes the average person to the Bible in ways that might be attractive but are naive. Let me offer some brief examples.

It is impossible to drive anywhere in the United States without turning on the car radio and hearing radio evangelists preach their message—often one of fire and brimstone and the evils of our day. Television evangelists are also prominent. Most are fundamentalist in their approach to the Bible and Christianity, and some offer strongly anti-Catholic messages reminiscent of the more argumentative days of the Protestant Reformation.

There is another kind of biblical tyranny at work in our society. At the supermarket I regularly see tabloids with sensational headlines about how the Bible predicts a harsh winter, or contains a formula that will help people win the lottery, or has a hidden code that predicted certain world events such as the assassination of Israeli prime minister Yitzak Rabin, or predicts some catastrophe that is soon to befall southern California. (Why pick on California? Earthquakes, perhaps?) Even more specifically, the Bible is invoked to support capital punishment on the basis of the Old Testament notion of "an eye for an eye and a tooth for a tooth," or to oppose women in the workplace or in politics because the Bible says they belong in the home. People flaunt the Bible's authority as the direct will of God that must be slavishly followed to the letter, albeit selectively interpreted, of course.

Catholics at times find themselves at a loss to explain to non-Catholic friends why our Church is the way it is when it does not seem outwardly to conform to the Bible. Why do we have a pope when the Bible doesn't mention the papacy at all? Why do Catholics "worship" Mary and the saints (we don't, but I'll explain that later) when the Bible says we should worship God alone? Why do Catholics address their priests as "father" when the Bible clearly prohibits this (more on that later, too)? In short, there is a pastoral reality that requires a reasoned response. We need more than a knee-jerk reaction to a phenomenon we don't understand and may fear. The Bible is used and misused regularly in our society, and Catholics should know more how to handle such situations knowledgeably.

Already in the 1980s the American bishops issued a statement acknowledging that Catholics were coming into contact with biblical fundamentalism and that this phenomenon posed an urgent pastoral problem. (See the bibliography.) In many instances, the seemingly logical simplicity of biblical fundamentalism was irresistible. Catholics in the United States and abroad have been attracted away from the Church and drawn into fundamentalist communities. The Catholic bishops in Latin America, for example, have been alarmed at the number of Catholics who have joined Evangelical fundamentalist groups. The same can be said for parts of Africa.

This book aims to provide a concise but thorough response to questions that Catholics have about fundamentalism. This book is not about fundamentalism in general, as it might be described in many different world religions (e.g., fundamentalist Muslims or Jews), but about Christian biblical fundamentalism. The purpose is threefold: (1) to offer instruction on the origins and main ideas of biblical fundamentalism, (2) to compare and contrast a Catholic perspective on the Bible with that of fundamentalists, and (3) to offer practical advice and recommend resources to assist Catholics in responding to fundamentalism.

The book has five chapters. The first chapter explains the historical origins of Christian biblical fundamentalism and why it is in its current form a uniquely American phenomenon. Fundamentalism is a word that can be used to describe many different phenomena. It is important to know what specifically is meant by biblical fundamentalism, where it came from, and why it exists. The second chapter outlines the main tenets of fundamentalist faith and how it approaches the Bible. The third chapter does the same for a Catholic perspective on the Bible, or as we sometimes call it, sacred Scripture. In my experience, many Catholics are rather limited in their understanding of Church teaching on the Bible. If Catholics are to become comfortable with God's written Word, they must first know what their Church teaches about

xiv   *Biblical Fundamentalism*

the Bible and how to read it. The fourth chapter offers an explanation of why biblical fundamentalism is attractive in our day, and a critique of it. I aim for a non-polemical evaluation of fundamentalism that recognizes its strengths and its weaknesses. Finally, the fifth chapter imparts some practical advice about how to fashion a sensible Catholic response to fundamentalism. A short bibliography of selected resources for further study will provide direction to those who wish to explore this topic on their own in more depth.

1

The Origins of Biblical Fundamentalism

Biblical fundamentalism is a multi-faceted phenomenon that did not emerge in a vacuum. It has long historical roots that have shaped its existence. To appreciate its complexity, we need to describe it accurately, discern its origins, and understand why it came into being.

What is biblical fundamentalism and what are its origins?

Fundamentalism is a more complex reality than would be readily apparent from observing radio or television evangelists. Yet there is a basic description of biblical fundamentalism, probably familiar to most people, that is generally applicable and accepted by fundamentalists themselves. George Marsden, a prominent Protestant theologian and an expert on the fundamentalist movement, offers the following description of fundamentalism at its roots:

> . . . [a] militantly anti-modernist Protestant evangelicalism
> . . . a loose, diverse, and changing federation of co-belligerents
> united by their fierce opposition to modernist attempts to
> bring Christianity in line with modern thought (Marsden,
> *Fundamentalism and American Culture,* 4).

He also has a shorthand version of describing a fundamentalist as "an evangelical who is angry about something" (Cohen, *The Fundamentalist Phenomenon*, 22). Marsden emphasizes that while other elements such as evangelism, prayer, personal holiness, and the giving of missions also characterize fundamentalism, its distinctiveness lies in its militant opposition to modernity. Jerry Falwell, the well-known fundamentalist Baptist religious leader who founded the Moral Majority in the late 1970s, and his colleagues agree with this characterization of fundamentalism as the "twentieth-century movement closely tied to the revivalist tradition of mainstream Evangelical Protestantism that militantly opposed modernist theology and the cultural change associated with it" (Falwell, *The Fundamentalist Phenomenon*, 3). Essentially, fundamentalists see themselves as defending authentic Christian religion against the evils of modern life. Modernity is the big enemy. It sabotages traditional Christian values and must be opposed militantly by a core of faithful Christians. It is, in short, a vehicle for Satan who opposes all that is decent and good.

Almost every word in Marsden's concise definition is important for understanding fundamentalism. The *militant* aspect helps to explain the desire of fundamentalists to become active in political change and to strategize and organize carefully. They see themselves as the army of God defending truth and the American way (as they perceive it). It is paradoxical that certain American values are tied up with fundamentalism (individualism, freedom, etc.). It purports to operate strictly from a biblical perspective, but sociologically and politically fundamentalism is intimately tied to American culture. Much of the modern thought opposed by fundamentalists grows out of the American way of life. The *anti-modernist* stance explains the fundamentalist tendency to oppose modern developments and to idealize the past. They particularly idealize the early Christian community as described in the New Testament, especially in the Acts of the Apostles. In their view modern developments have corrupted the original pristine Christian organization. Fundamentalists believe they must return the Christian community to the purer ways of the earliest days of Christian existence. Back to the "fundamentals" is their battle cry. "Give me that ol' time religion" is another favorite slogan.

The *Protestant Evangelical* character of fundamentalism is also important. Experts who have studied fundamentalisms around the world have noted the unique character of American biblical fundamentalism rooted, not just in Protestant thought in general, but in Evangelical Christianity. One should note, however, that while all fundamentalists are Evangelical, not all Evangelicals are fundamentalists. Evangelical Christianity, which comprises some 25 percent of Protestant groups in the United States, encompasses a wide spectrum of approaches to the Bible. Some are Pentecostals who emphasize the work of the Holy Spirit in their lives and the charismatic gifts that come with being filled with the Spirit, such as healing, prophecy, and speaking in tongues (technically called "glossolalia"). Others are "holiness" groups, such as the Church of the Nazarene and the Church of God, that emphasize certain individual and revivalist aspects of Christian faith. Still others are individual congregations of Baptists, Disciples of Christ, and others from mainline Protestant groups who identify themselves as fundamentalist in their approach to the Bible and to religion. Some Evangelicals accept modern scientific study of the Bible in ways fundamentalists do not. But many fundamentalist doctrines emerged from traditional Evangelical teachings.

Furthermore, fundamentalism has been influenced by other Protestant phenomena closely associated with it, such as pietism, revivalism, millenarianism, and Baptist traditionalism. All have left their mark on the fundamentalist movement but are not directly identified with it. The fact that fundamentalism is a *loose, diverse, and changing* movement points out its highly individualistic character. Many different groups fit themselves under the large umbrella category of fundamentalism. Each congregation tends to define itself, and there is no overarching authority that governs fundamentalist communities. It can also be difficult to categorize some groups because of the loose boundaries that are used to distinguish fundamentalists from other Evangelicals.

Finally, their *opposition to reconciling Christianity with modernity* has made them often appear to be anti-intellectual and separatist, and in some extreme forms that is patently so. Since in their view modernity corrupts, some fundamentalists believe the only acceptable response they can give is to remove themselves from society. They base their view on their interpretation of certain passages from the Bible that call for separation from unbelievers (e.g., 2 Cor 6:14-18; Rom 12:1-2). The notion that Christianity is anti-rationalist and anti-humanistic is a driving force in fundamentalist perspective that can strike outsiders as quaint, at best, or dangerously naive, at worst.

I must call the reader's attention to another caution as we proceed. Defining fundamentalism and its extent can be tricky business. This is so for historical as well as theological reasons. Throughout its history, the fundamentalist movement has had a tendency to splinter into various factions with the result that some are more conservative and some more liberal, introducing internal controversies over self-identity. Baptists, the largest Protestant denomination in the United States, are a case in point. Some Baptists clearly fall into the fundamentalist network by virtue of their approach to the Bible and other doctrinal issues. Yet other Baptists could not be classified as fundamentalists and would object to such a categorization. The large Southern Baptist Convention, for example, has its own internal disagreements about such issues. It can be difficult to decide just who belongs where on the spectrum of fundamentalism. For that matter, some Baptists debate whether or not they belong within Evangelical Christianity or whether they would be better categorized under a different heading. Self-designation is one criteria for describing fundamentalists, but I believe there are also other objective criteria that can be used. At the risk of some over-simplification, I offer the following historical sketch of the development of biblical fundamentalism within American Protestantism because it helps to see how it became a natural outgrowth of American culture.

The roots of fundamentalism stretch back to the eighteenth century. In the wake of the scientific exploration of the world that began with the Enlightenment, some Christians felt threatened by the new knowledge that seemed to undermine the essentials of Christian existence. Scientific study of the Bible began to question even the literal veracity of some of the biblical data. Before this time, the Bible had been taken quite literally to be factual in everything that it said. Scientific study began to see inconsistencies in the Bible that called into question the nature of the biblical material. The uneven seams of the biblical texts which gave evidence of their origin in a complex process of oral, written, and edited traditions over many centuries began to erode confidence in "gospel truth." Human reason began to be exalted over religion. A primary religious influence in America in this time period was Evangelical Protestantism. It mainly showed itself in three forms, Calvinism, Puritanism, and Revivalism. All of these religious traditions, in their own ways, tried to preserve (or restore) Christian values as they perceived them to be.

In the nineteenth century, despite their attempts to win adherents, several factors led to the decline of the influence of Evangelical Christians. The rise of the Industrial Revolution and all that came with it had a major impact on American life. New immigrants came to America, many of them Catholic, Jewish, and Lutheran who had different religious perspectives. The rise of various industries and the urbanization that accompanied it began to influence dramatically the pace and direction of life. America was quickly being transformed from a largely rural, agricultural society into a modern, secularized urban one. In addition, the scientific arena, in the person of Charles Darwin and his theory of evolution, began to produce new, controversial theories about the origins of human life itself. His famous treatise *Origin of Species* (1859) created a huge stir that some characterized glibly as asserting that human beings descended from monkeys. The biblical perspective of creation expressed by the book of Genesis seemed under direct attack. It eroded even the acceptance of Adam and Eve as historical figures.

Indeed, the rise of the historical-critical study of the Bible earlier in the nineteenth century had already begun to influence this trend. The expression "historical-critical" is a translation of a German term that means the objective, scientific study of the biblical text within its historical context. In 1835 a biblical scholar named David Friedrich Strauss published a book entitled *The Life of Jesus Critically Examined* that asserted that the New Testament contained "mythical" elements invented by the early Church to embellish the life of Jesus. This meant that the Gospels could not be trusted at face value in a literal, factual way. So not only was the Old Testament suspect, but the Gospels themselves came under scientific scrutiny.

The exploration of "myth" and "theology" in the Bible began to impact scientific biblical studies. According to scientific theories about the Bible, the historical kernel of truth embedded in it was shrouded in other extraneous elements that reflected the faith of the early Church rather than bedrock factual tradition. Historical certitude took a back seat to other priorities. Historical skepticism grew even about the most fundamental of Judeo-Christian beliefs. To Evangelical Christians, all of this was due to the influence of a secular, pluralistic society. They felt they were witnessing the erosion of "traditional" values that were replaced by humanistic ones. Moreover, liberalism in the mainline Protestant churches was on the rise in the late nineteenth century and into the twentieth century. Liberal Protestants preferred to shift the focus of Christian faith away from doctrinal and biblical truths to social action. Evangelicals began to feel that American Protestantism itself was losing its moral compass and was straying from the truth.

By the twentieth century some Evangelical Christians felt that this secular, humanistic trend had gone far enough. Something dramatic was needed to correct the misdirection of the country and to resurrect the "ol' time religion" of a bygone era. Between 1910 and 1915 two wealthy Californians (originally from Pennsylvania), Milton and Lyman Stewart, financed the publication of a series of twelve paperback pamphlets called *The Fundamentals of the Christian Religion* (shortened to *The Fundamentals*). These contained ninety articles, twenty-seven of them devoted to the Bible, which outlined clearly what were thought to be the essential, fundamental beliefs of Christianity that could not be compromised. (An edited version is available as *The Fundamentals: The Famous Sourcebook of Foundational Biblical Truths*, R. A. Torrey, ed. [Grand Rapids, Mich.: Kregel, 1990].) Two of the articles also dealt with the evils of Roman Catholicism and why it did not represent authentic Christian faith. In 1920 a Northern Baptist journalist by the name of Curtis Lee Laws coined the term "fundamentalist" in referring to those who adhered to these fundamental religious doctrines, and a Baptist group assumed the label as a self-designation. The name has stuck ever since.

This is obviously a thumbnail sketch of a much more complicated history of biblical fundamentalism than can be recounted here. Yet it provides sufficient data to demonstrate its American roots and the tendencies that still characterize it as a contemporary religious movement.

Fundamentalists are usually proud of the designation, although some resent the term as derogatory. A dictionary definition of fundamentalism proposes two aspects of the label, one specific and one generic. The first definition speaks broadly of "A Protestant movement characterized by a belief in the literal truth of the Bible." The second and more generic description is: "A movement or point of view characterized by rigid adherence to fundamental or basic principles" (*The American Heritage Dictionary*, 2nd college ed. [Boston: Houghton Mifflin, 1991] 539). In common parlance, however, fundamentalism has come to mean a narrow, rigid, conservative, highly opinionated, and often uneducated adherence to outdated, non-scientific, anti-intellectual perspectives. Our analysis of fundamentalism in this book primarily addresses the first definition, not the generic one. Scholars, in fact, disagree whether or not the expression "fundamentalist" ought to be applied analogously to other groups that might better be characterized as rigid dogmatists or traditionalists. For better or worse, the name fundamentalist has come to mean anyone who is rigid and inflexible. That is why one *can* speak of fundamentalists of the right or the left. We will focus, however, on the specific American Protestant fundamentalist movement that continues to wield considerable influence at the beginning of the twenty-first century.

The Evangelical biblical scholar Cyrus I. Scofield (1843–1921) gave authoritative impetus to the fundamentalist movement in 1909 by the publication of a Bible, *The Scofield Reference Bible* (New York: Oxford University, 1909; 2nd ed. 1917), which defended the Authorized King James Version as the only reliable English Bible translation. The King James Version was originally published in 1611 using as a translation source the Hebrew and Greek manuscripts available at the time. The Scofield edition of it provided extensive explanatory notes to interpret the Bible in clear terms according to fundamentalist principles. In particular, it presents a dispensationalist reading of the Bible (described below in chapter 4) that has become characteristic of biblical fundamentalism. Although this Bible has undergone three revisions since that time, it remains *the* authoritative Bible translation and source book for fundamentalists, and its translation remains virtually the same as the original seventeenth-century one. The third edition, completed by a team of fundamentalist scholars, adds considerable amounts of interpretation to the text, edits some of the archaic language of the translation, and expands some of the interpretation from the original version, but it retains the basic direction of the original (see *The New Scofield Study Bible,* 3rd ed. [New York: Oxford University, 1967]).

A real watershed event for the fundamentalist movement came quickly in 1925 with the infamous Scopes "monkey trial" held in Dayton, Tennessee. This dramatic legal confrontation between the famous lawyers William Jennings Bryon and Clarence Darrow, artistically portrayed by the 1955 play (and 1960 movie) *Inherit the Wind,* brought to the forefront of the American public the clash between modernity and fundamentalists. The trial concerned a high school teacher, John Thomas Scopes (1900–1970), who was convicted of teaching the scientific theory of evolution in opposition to the biblical teaching of creation, contrary to Tennessee law. The conviction was later overturned, but the trial focused national attention on the rise of fundamentalism and its literal approach to the Bible. In the popular imagination this trial has become the symbolic defining event for American biblical fundamentalism. As one fundamentalist characterized the importance of the trial's outcome, "Monkey origins means monkey morals."

Throughout the entire development of fundamentalist religion, there has been a tendency to splinter into various groups. Hence the complexity of the phenomenon. Without getting into unnecessary details, we can say that fundamentalism consists of many independent Protestant Evangelical communities who are united primarily in their opposition to modern, liberal, and secular influence in society. Although they have similar approaches to the Bible, they are split on the interpretation of some aspects of Scripture. In particular, they have disagreed over how to interpret the millennium, the one-thousand-year reign of Christ described in the book of Revelation (20:2-7). Some fundamentalists have been amillennialists, meaning that the thousand-year reign is more symbolic of Christ's victory over Satan than it is literal. Others have been postmillennialists, meaning that Christ's reign will occur *after* a thousand-year period of peace and prosperity has returned to the earth. Still others, who hold to the dominant current perspective among fundamentalists, are premillennialists who believe Christ will return in glory to re-establish the true Israel *before* the thousand-year reign of prosperity, in order to inaugurate it. All fundamentalists, however, are united in the need forcefully to evangelize the world and bring about an authentic moral conversion to Jesus Christ so that people will be saved.

What are the "fundamentals"?

As their name implies, fundamentalists are concerned about the "fundamentals" of the Christian faith. At the heart of their teaching is the belief that certain core doctrines are essential to Christian faith. These were expounded in the pamphlets called *The Fundamentals*. In the view of fundamentalists, these truths are so basic and necessary that they must be adhered to forcefully and without compromise. They point to five, in particular.

(1) Uppermost in the hierarchy of fundamentalist beliefs is that the *Bible is inerrant* in all that it teaches. That is to say, the Bible contains no errors. We will explore this topic more thoroughly in the next chapter. Here we need only point out that this belief emphasizes that, because the Bible is God's Word, it cannot possibly contain any error whatsoever, even historical or scientific errors, let alone theological ones.

(2) The *virginal conception and birth of Jesus* is another central tenet of fundamentalist faith. This is essential to preserve the understanding that Jesus Christ was God.

(3) A third belief is that, by his suffering and death on the cross, Jesus Christ made *substitutionary penal atonement* for human sinfulness. His sole action redeemed the world and offers salvation to all who would embrace him as the messiah, Son of God. He alone atones for human sinfulness. He is the one who died for all humanity; he is our "substitute" who redeems our wickedness.

(4) A belief in the physical, *bodily resurrection of Jesus* is also crucial to fundamentalist faith. The resurrection of Jesus is God's ultimate act of vindication of Jesus' claim to be the messiah, God's own Son. This doctrine is importantly tied to the belief that the dead will also be raised bodily when Christ returns in glory to establish God's final kingdom.

(5) Finally, belief in the parousia (from Greek *parousia*, "coming"), or the literal *second coming of Christ* to judge the world, is central. Many fundamentalists go so far as to explain in detail the physical return of Christ to the earth, how they must prepare for it, and what will happen to faithful believers and to unrepentant sinners when Jesus returns in glory. In their jargon, this is called "the rapture," based upon an obscure passage in St. Paul (1 Thess 4:16-17) that we will examine later.

We should note that, with the exception of the first doctrine which has many implications for biblical interpretation, these quintessential fundamentalist beliefs are shared by most Christians, albeit from a variety of positions and with differences of interpretation or descriptive language. Even within fundamentalism there are variations of approach to the meaning of these doctrines. The fear of fundamentalists, however, is that modern liberal thought has undermined these essential doctrines by overemphasis on scientific, rational explanations, especially about the way the Bible is interpreted. Therefore they defend their views by reference to biblical authority. Since the Bible is taken to be God's Word, fundamentalists obviously view biblical teaching as the final word on the matter. It is difficult to get a higher authority than God! That is why their view of sacred Scripture is so critical to understand and provides the focal point of this book.

Principles of fundamentalist faith

These fundamental beliefs are accompanied by some important principles that derive from them and dictate the way fundamentalists operate. I enumerate six of them.

(1) The Bible provides the sole authority for Christian living. The Bible is capable of mediating God's will plainly. Anyone who takes the Bible in hand can receive God's direct unmediated message accurately. No intermediary is necessary. Some fundamentalist communities refuse to call themselves a "church," preferring an alternative like "assembly" or "community." To their mind, the very notion of church evokes a highly structured, authoritarian organization that is external to the gospel of Jesus Christ. There is no need for the Church or any other external authority to help interpret the will of God from the Bible. Some even view official churches as a hindrance to salvation and church officials as unnecessary, at best, or sheer obstacles to salvation, at worst. Emphasis is on individual faith. God's Spirit charismatically raises up leaders who get well versed in the Bible and are able to preach the Word of God effectively, thus bringing others to the faith.

(2) Eternal salvation comes only through the atonement achieved by Jesus Christ. That is why it is so crucial to be able to claim Jesus Christ as one's personal Lord and Savior. Most fundamentalists call themselves "born again Christians." They believe that they take to heart the message of Jesus in John's Gospel to be "born again" (John 3:3) and

identify this act of conversion with a specific time and place when one literally and verbally assents to Jesus Christ as one's personal Lord and Savior. There are seven specific steps to being "born again" (see Eric Gritsch, *Born Again-ism: Perspectives on a Movement* [Philadelphia: Fortress, 1982] 91–92):

- explicit acknowledgment of one's sinfulness
- repentance and direct renunciation of sin
- inviting the Lord Jesus into one's life to redirect it
- surrender to God's will
- defeating one's suffering and overcoming one's problems
- experiencing God's direct care
- acceptance *now* of the salvation God extends.

These actions are thought to transform one's life totally once and for all.

(3) Every Christian must evangelize (from Greek, *euag-gelizomai*, "proclaim good news") the world by personal testimony. Because the gospel message is so crucial to salvation, everyone who has received the message bears a responsibility to carry it forth to others. Fundamentalists are thus very evangelical in their faith. They see the need to evangelize the world, to save all humanity from sin. They cannot sit back but must actively engage in spreading the message of Jesus to the whole world. Many fundamentalist groups are adept at missionary work in developing countries such as in South America or Africa where they have made great strides in converting people to their faith. They also have a great concern for the conversion of Jews and other non-Christians whom they wish to bring into the fold of Christ.

(4) Every Christian must lead a strictly moral life. This is usually accompanied by strict prohibitions against smoking, dancing, consuming alcohol or drugs, gambling, card playing, etc. One thinks of the slogan, "We don't smoke nor drink nor chew, and we don't go with girls who do." This attitude, of course, does not make them immune to sin. As with most denominations, there have been prominent scandals when some of their ministerial leadership were caught in adultery or other immoral activities. (One thinks of the

sexual scandals of Jimmy Swaggert or Jim Bakker in the late twentieth century.) Sometimes this strict moral code even goes so far as to avoid participation in some standard public events such as Halloween (associated with Satan worship, witches, etc.), having Christmas trees at Christmas (associated with pagan ritual), or reading the Harry Potter stories of J. K. Rowling (associated with witchcraft and wizardry).

(5) Christians must be uncompromising and militant in preserving the truth. Fundamentalists see themselves as guardians of the true Christian faith. They must, therefore, militantly oppose everything they think goes counter to authentic Christianity. They often employ the language of war and battle. (Remember "Onward! Christian Soldiers"? It was composed in England in 1864 as a marching song to lend a sense of strong commitment to the Christian message.) Fundamentalists are engaged in a cosmic war between good and evil. They oppose modern critical study of the Bible, secularization, and humanism because these attack basic Christian values and actually destroy them. Even within their own organizations some fundamentalist denominations have been severely fractured by infighting when it was perceived that leadership was not holding the line against outside negative influences. Some fundamentalist groups have decided simply to opt out of society in order to preserve authentic faith. These separatists sometimes set up home schooling for their children so that they will not be corrupted by mainstream American values. One should note, though, that some fundamentalists view their extreme counterparts as "hyper-fundamentalists" because of their excessive rigidity and their exaggerated separatist tendency.

(6) Finally, most fundamentalists have a particular eschatological view (from Greek, *eschaton,* "end time") about the events that will take place at the end of time. They eagerly await and anticipate soon the second coming of Jesus. Their eschatological perspective adds urgency to their message, for they feel the time is short and they are called to advance the spread of Jesus' message as far and wide as they can before the climactic events of the end time take place. For this principle, fundamentalists rely on certain key passages of the

Bible that focus on apocalyptic (from Greek, *apokalypsis,* "revelation, unveiling") expectations, such as the book of Revelation. Their interpretations of these passages sometimes project very detailed scenarios of what will take place when God finally establishes the eternal kingdom.

These six operative principles are foundational to fundamentalism and give practical direction to the efforts to spread their message.

Fundamentalisms of the world

Before moving to a more thorough exploration of the fundamentalist approach to the Bible, I should say a word about fundamentalism in other parts of the world. Often public media speak of other types of fundamentalism that are current and that have strong political leanings. At times, for instance, radical Muslim or Jewish "fundamentalists" in other countries capture the headlines when they make dramatic declarations or even are involved in violent, terrorist activities. Is there a connection to biblical fundamentalism?

The response to this question is both yes and no. Affirmatively, one may point to certain similarities in any religious fundamentalism, regardless of the denominational leaning. Professor Martin E. Marty, an expert church historian, points to eleven common elements that can be found in "fundamentalist" groups ("Fundamentals of Fundamentalism," 18–23):

- origins in traditional and conservative cultures
- a vague sense of being threatened from outside forces
- unease and discontent with life
- a defensive and reactive posture
- movement toward separatism from others
- a desperate search for authority
- an intentional desire to scandalize those who are outsiders
- resistance to ambivalence and ambiguity
- creation of a sharply defined dualistic culture
- a tendency toward aggression in order to foster their perspective

- collapsing the future into the present by their exaggerated view of future victory.

These characteristics show up in various types of fundamentalism around the world. Recent anthropological and sociological studies affirm certain common connections among fundamentalists. Fundamentalists of any stripe rely upon defined sacred texts that invoke divine authority. Thus Muslims have their Koran and Jews have their Tanak or Hebrew Bible. There are fundamentalists in these religions who analogously read their "bible" as American fundamentalists read the Bible. The typical fundamentalist approach to such sacred texts is to read them from a literal perspective. Often the text undergirds certain political positions or aspirations, and again from their perspective, divine authority is hard to contradict. If God dictates a "holy war," then so be it. That is the cost of defending the truth.

Additionally, there is another reality that might better be termed traditionalism or dogmatism that is tied to fundamentalism. This is more a psychological tendency to operate in an absolute, apodictic way that allows little room for compromise or flexibility. Certain preconceived dogmatic positions guide one's actions, and no amount of reasoning will deter one from this chosen direction. To be sure, elements of psychological rigidity show up in all forms of fundamentalism. I mentioned above that fundamentalism of this stripe can show up on either side of the political spectrum, from the left or the right, the liberal or the conservative.

Yet the negative part of the proposition is that unique political realities govern many fundamentalist phenomena around the world that are so diverse that they defy easy categorization. No analysis can explain uniformly every facet of fundamentalism. Careful sociological scrutiny requires an exploration of the special circumstances that guide each type of fundamentalism. This book is neither a sociological/ anthropological nor a psychological study. It is first and foremost a book on Bible instruction with a view toward aiding a comparison and contrast between the typical fundamentalist and non-fundamentalist approaches to the Bible, and to compare a fundamentalist stance toward the Bible with a Catholic one.

Consequently, I will not attempt to address fundamentalism as a universal religious phenomenon. Other experts have explored this territory in sophisticated studies (see the multivolume work *The Fundamentalisms Project* in the bibliography). Rather, I will keep a more modest focus on the Protestant American biblical fundamentalism that remains current in the U.S. and that has been exported to many other areas of the world by exuberant Evangelical Christians. This is the specific brand of fundamentalism that Catholics are likely to encounter and that causes concerns. Let's turn now to the cornerstone of biblical fundamentalism, how to read the Bible.

2

Bible Basics: A Fundamentalist Approach to Scripture

The interpretation of the Bible is where fundamentalism often clashes with other Christians. Biblical fundamentalists have developed a distinctive approach to Scripture within the Protestant sphere that must be understood before we can compare it with a Catholic approach. This chapter outlines the main characteristics of this approach to the Bible.

Principles for biblical interpretation

The main principle that fundamentalists adhere to in biblical interpretation is that the Bible is the sole authority on what God says and desires. The Bible alone is a sufficient resource for moral direction. Several corollaries accompany this principle. First, the Bible contains *all* you need to know. There is no need to supplement it with other doctrines or beliefs. Second, the Bible says exactly what it means and means what it says. There is no need for outside mediation to explain what the Bible teaches; its teaching is self-evident. The meaning rests in the actual words, and everyone who can read can understand its plain sense. Third, since the Bible is the Word of God, it must be inerrant; i.e., it contains no errors of any kind. This corollary is based upon a three-part logical syllogism that can be formulated thus:

> Major Premise: God cannot err.
> Minor premise: The Bible is the Word of God.
> Conclusion: Therefore, the Bible cannot err.

This is a logical construct in the fundamentalist system. Furthermore, if the Bible were to err even in the slightest matter, its truth would be totally compromised. Unfaithful in little things, more unfaithful in bigger things! A fourth corollary is that the moral authority of the Bible remains valid for all time. There can be no compromising on that authority. Finally, fundamentalists believe that the prophetic force of Scripture was intended directly for our own time, regardless of its original historical setting.

This main principle and its attendant corollaries are interrelated and reveal a particular approach to four concepts that are key to reading the Bible: authority (and the canon), inspiration, hermeneutics, and prophecy. Each of these requires some treatment.

Authority

The position that the Bible is the sole authority dates back to the days of the sixteenth-century Reformation of Martin Luther and others. The slogan of *sola scriptura* (Latin, "by scripture alone") became a hallmark of the Reformers' approach to Christian faith in comparison to the Catholic Church's assertion of the importance of its magisterial teaching through history. This phrase stood alongside two other Latin expressions that emphasize the Protestant reliance solely on God (*sola fide,* "by faith alone," and *sola gratia,* "by grace alone"). Fundamentalists are hard pressed, however, to point to any passage in the Bible itself where the assertion is made that it alone suffices for moral guidance. Indeed, some fundamentalists acknowledge that nowhere does the Bible itself claim this particular sole authority, yet they maintain it as a basic principle.

The passages that self-consciously refer to the sacred writings themselves are few and far between. Three passages stand out. One example is the magnificent passage of Isaiah which reads:

> For as the rain and the snow come down from heaven, and do not return there until they have watered the earth, making it bring forth and sprout, giving seed to the sower and bread to the eater, so shall my word be that goes out from my mouth; it shall not return to me empty, but it shall accomplish that which I purpose, and succeed in the thing for which I sent it (Isa 55:10-11).

This highly poetic passage from the anonymous prophet of the Babylonian Exile called Second Isaiah speaks of the efficacy of God's Word. We must note, however, that a fundamentalist position would not acknowledge the composite nature of the book of Isaiah. Most scholars, whether Protestant, Catholic, or Jewish, believe that the book of Isaiah actually consists of the prophecies of three prophets from three different time periods in Israel's history, Isaiah of Jerusalem (eighth cent. B.C.) and two anonymous prophets who date from later periods (sixth–fifth cent. B.C.) and who are designated Second and Third Isaiah. Scribes combined these materials into one book because of the similarities of the prophetic outlook and the themes of the prophecies. It is also possible that the later anonymous prophets styled themselves consciously in the image of the great eighth-century prophet Isaiah. In any case, the book is of a composite nature.

In the context of Isaiah 55:1-13, the message of the present passage concerns the promise of God to restore the chosen people after their time in exile. God's Word is compared to the rain and snow that come from the sky and make the land fertile. God's Word is faithful; it has promised to restore Israel and it will be done. Just as water transforms the desert into a garden, so shall God's Word transform the barren, dejected people of Israel once more into a joyous nation. The main message, then, is that God's Word can be trusted. God speaks, God's will is done. Promising the efficacy of God's Word says nothing about whether God uses other means to accomplish the divine will, in addition to the Word. This passage simply asserts that God's Word is effective. The other two major passages that consciously speak of Scripture concern inspiration, to which we will turn shortly below.

Authority and the canon

Another important aspect of authority is the notion of the canon. All Christians consider the Bible to be canonical literature. The concept of the canon is derived from Greek (*kanōn,* "measuring rod or norm"). It implies that the Bible can be used as a means to measure one's spiritual and moral progress. To call the Bible a canon is to accept it as a collection of authoritative works used to direct one's life. Along with other Christians, fundamentalists clearly acknowledge this canonical function of Scripture, but they view the origin of the canon in a non-historical fashion. They assert the existence of the canon but not the process of its formation. Many fundamentalists think of the formation of the Bible as a revealed reality, as if it suddenly appeared on the human scene with its divine message intact. They are not so naive as to think that the Bible literally dropped out of heaven but that the original authors were somehow guided by God to write every word with infallible accuracy, thus producing an infallible text.

Most biblical scholars, whether Protestant or Catholic, recognize the complex origins of the Christian canon of sacred Scripture. The Old and New Testament writings evolved over thousands of years in a process that included oral, written, and collected and edited traditions which inevitably allowed accretions to creep in. The community of Christians, the Church itself, had to make a decision at some point about which books were to be considered canonical and which were to be excluded. Most scholars believe that the New Testament canon was finished definitively by the fourth century A.D., around the time of St. Athanasius, bishop of Alexandria (ca. A.D. 367, the date of his thirty-ninth festal letter at Easter, which lists the canon of Scripture as we have it). This process is important for interpretation because it allows for explanations of contradictions and the historical development of different moral perspectives over time, something that the fundamentalist approach to the Bible ignores.

They do not acknowledge that the Church formed the canon of sacred Scripture under the guidance of the Holy Spirit.

We should note also that the formation of the canon was not entirely arbitrary. There were some accepted criteria that the Church used to determine what books to incorporate into the canon and what ones to exclude. Among the criteria were the supposed apostolic authorship of the texts, the accepted antiquity of the writings, their widespread public use among various Christian communities, their presumed inspiration as sacred texts, their general consistency with one another, and the accepted doctrinal perspective on Jesus Christ. The process, however, was not always smooth and led to disagreements, some of which endured for centuries. At certain points, the Church made a decision to exclude from the canon such early Christian works as the Didache, the Letters of Ignatius of Antioch, and the Shepherd of Hermas, along with the more suspect apocryphal Gospels. Our main point here is to emphasize the long, involved development of the Christian canon which fundamentalists tend to ignore.

Inspiration

The Bible's canonical authority rests on the assertion that it is inspired literature. Its unique origin lies with God who is the ultimate author of the contents of the Bible. For fundamentalists, the most important passage for the scriptural authority of the Bible comes from 2 Timothy, which says:

> All scripture is inspired by God and is useful for teaching, for reproof, for correction, and for training in righteousness, so that everyone who belongs to God may be proficient, equipped for every good work (3:16-17).

The reason for granting to the Bible this unique authority is because it is deemed by all Christians to be uniquely inspired literature. No other literature has the same authority. The beauty and truth contained in the writings of William Shakespeare, Robert Frost, or your favorite author may be *inspiring*, but such literature is not considered *inspired*. Let's look at this notion of inspiration more carefully.

All Christians believe the Bible to be the inspired Word of God. They hold to what is called the "doctrine of inspiration." Asserting *that* the Bible is inspired is not the same thing as saying *how* this inspiration works or is accomplished. Just what does the passage in Second Timothy say? Several observations are important.

First, note that the expression "all scripture" (Greek, *pasa graphē*) refers to the scriptures familiar to the audience for whom the letter was written (cf. also the expression "according to the scriptures" in 1 Cor 15:3, 4). At the time this letter was composed, the New Testament did not yet exist as a collection of authoritative works. (The authorship of the letter is disputed. Most scholars date it ca. A.D. 64–68 or 80–90, depending on whether it was composed by early disciples of Paul or later ones, writing in his name. Most scholars doubt that Paul himself wrote the letter.) In other words, the reference to scriptures is to what Christians call the Old Testament (the Hebrew Bible), which for the early Christians was the authoritative Scripture as they knew it. Later Christian interpretation, of course, acknowledged that all Scripture considered canonical would derive this same authority. That is why the passage can now apply to both Testaments of the Bible.

Second, the adjective "inspired" (Greek, *theopneustos*) literally means "God-breathed." It only occurs once in the entire Bible in this very passage. Just as in the English root "inspire" (breath into), so the Greek root asserts that God has breathed life or meaning into these words called Scripture. They contain God's Spirit. God stands behind the writings as the ultimate author, though working through the human authors. The word "inspired" does not contain any hidden meaning as to how inspiration is accomplished. Nor does it resolve the "what" of inspiration. Is it the oral or written word? The Hebrew or Greek words? The translations? The expression merely asserts that God is the source of these words. God is the ultimate author. Thus the sacred writings contain the message God intended.

Finally, the passage outlines why having inspired literature is important. It is useful (Greek, *ōphelimos*, "useful, beneficial, advantageous") for a variety of Christian tasks: teaching, reproof, correction, and instruction in righteousness. The goal is the formation of an upright Christian. The Bible is useful in this regard. Despite its unique inspired status, the Bible never claims to be the sole source for Christian formation. Rather, by means of instruction and being morally redirected to live a righteous life, Scripture is a reliable guide, a useful resource. Indeed, all Christians would deem the Bible indispensable for authentic Christian living. Yet the passage does not explain exactly how inspiration works nor does it defend the principle of *sola scriptura*.

Another passage that fundamentalists use to explain their stance on inspiration is found in 2 Peter:

> First of all you must understand this, that no prophecy of scripture is a matter of one's own interpretation, because no prophecy ever came by human will, but men and women moved by the Holy Spirit spoke from God (1:20-21).

Essentially, this passage says that prophetic utterances do not stem from human origin but divine. The "Holy Spirit" is the source of prophecy, and interpretation of it is not based upon an individual's understanding but upon God's meaning placed within the sacred writings. But we note here again that the passage does not explain how one arrives at a correct interpretation. To assert that the Holy Spirit is the source of Scripture and its authentic interpreter is compatible with the inspired nature of the Bible, but it does not resolve the "how" of interpretation. Interestingly, this passage also militates against personal interpretation, something that is a hallmark of a fundamentalist approach.

Since the doctrine of inspiration is an essential part of all Christian denominations, it is not surprising that each has grappled with trying to determine how inspiration works. Fundamentalists accept the theory of "plenary verbal inspiration." This means that every single word of the autograph editions of the Bible (i.e., the originals) is fully inspired and inerrant. Fundamentalists understand their theory of inspiration according to three principles:

1) The Bible is verbally inspired; i.e., not just the message is inspired but the words themselves are inspired.
2) The Bible is plenarily inspired; i.e., the words are not merely human words but God's Word, fully containing the message that God intended.
3) The Bible is wholly inerrant; i.e., it is utterly infallible.

One should note, by the way, that the terms "inerrant" and "infallible" are used synonymously. Some Protestants rather sarcastically refer to the use of the Bible in an overly authoritarian fashion as the "paper pope," making the connection quite explicit. A fundamentalist spokesman summarizes inerrancy in this fashion:

> The Bible in all its parts constitutes the written Word of God to man [sic]. This Word is free from all error in its original autographs. . . . It is wholly trustworthy in matters of history and doctrine . . . [The] authors of Scripture, under the guidance of the Holy Spirit, were preserved from making factual, historical, scientific, or other errors (Harold Lindsell, *The Battle for the Bible* [Grand Rapids, Mich.: Eerdmans, 1976] 30–31).

The word "autograph" itself requires some explanation. Fundamentalists base their conviction on the existence of original manuscripts—as described, for example, in Jeremiah 36:1-32, which tells of Jeremiah's dictation of his words to his secretary Baruch—which were eventually lost in time. Since the autographs no longer exist, however, there is no way of reconstructing the original text with certainty. There are several thousand Greek manuscripts of the New Testament, for instance, but none of them is an original. They are all copies of copies written over centuries by scribes who were charged with preserving them and passing them on to future generations. The manuscripts, many of them in fragmentary state, date from around the second to the tenth centuries A.D., hundreds of years after the events that they recount. There is no foolproof means of determining what the autographs of these copies actually looked like, so there is a problem of determining the object of this notion of inspiration.

Although fundamentalists maintain the theory of plenary inspiration, few today hold to a "dictation theory" of inspiration in which God directly dictated the words to the human authors. The ability of scholars to examine manuscripts by means of "textual criticism" in which tiny differences of expression in the original languages can be tracked to scribal errors has shown the improbability of any dictation method. The author quoted above, Harold Lindsell, emphasizes the futility of a dictation theory, though he acknowledges that it is a theory that refuses to die among some ultra-conservative fundamentalists.

The theory of plenary verbal inspiration emphasizes the need for literal interpretation of the Bible, but not in every single instance. Thus, when the Bible says that the world was created in seven days (Gen 1:1–2:4), then it literally means in one week of twenty-four hour days as we understand it. When the Bible speaks of the walls of Jericho tumbling down at the sound of trumpet blasts and great shouts (Josh 6:1-20), then that is literally what happened. But when the Bible says "if your right eye causes you to sin tear it out and throw it away" (Matt 5:29) or "they will pick up snakes in their hands, and if they drink any deadly thing, it will not hurt them" (Mark 16:18), not all fundamentalists would take such advice literally. Fundamentalists also recognize use of figures of speech in the Bible such as symbol, metaphor, and hyperbole even while they hold to a more literal interpretation. Other Evangelicals and Protestants would adhere to a less stringent theory of inspiration, "limited verbal inspiration," relating the inerrancy of the Bible to matters of faith and morals rather than to history or science.

As the reader can see, explaining the doctrine of inspiration is tricky business. The fundamentalist attempts to explain *how* it operates leaves much to be desired. Acceptance of plenary verbal inspiration puts one in an awkward position to deal with contradictions in the Bible.

Hermeneutics

Application of the Bible is often at the heart of controversies over interpretation. How does one apply ancient texts to new and modern situations? Hermeneutics is a fancy word for "interpretation" (from Greek, *hermeneuō*). One could say that the really critical challenge for all Christians is learning how to interpret the Bible properly. Every age has had to struggle with how to apply the sacred Scriptures to their own era and their own lives. Just as with inspiration there are different theories, so with hermeneutics there are different approaches.

Hermeneutically, fundamentalists take a position that can be termed "direct transference." This means that the Bible can be directly applied on all matters, not only religious issues but also scientific and historical ones. A corollary to this approach is that the New Testament interprets the Old Testament and supersedes it in terms of ritual but not in terms of moral teaching. Again, other Evangelicals take a broader approach that says the Bible can be applied directly in matters of faith or morals but not in history or science.

Any passages that are unclear are interpreted by understanding passages that are clearer, so that contradictions are only apparent rather than real. Fundamentalists do some fancy footwork in interpretation to reconcile apparent contradictions in the Bible. Let's look at a few illustrations.

A good example is the approach to Genesis 1–2 in what most scholars view as two separate stories of creation written by different authors in different time periods. Most biblical scholars accept Genesis 1 as originating around the sixth century B.C. with a group of scribes who were concerned about the preservation of the liturgical traditions of the Jews (thus the concern for the seven-day schema of creation and the notion of the sabbath). Genesis 2, on the other hand, originates from an earlier, more primitive tradition dated to around the tenth century B.C. Fundamentalists, however, do not view the two stories as separate, the first one (Gen 1:1–2:4) being poetic and the second one (Gen 2:4-25) being more anthropomorphic, i.e., describing God in very human terms as a divine sculptor who forms the first human being out of dust. For fundamentalists, this is not a second story of creation but merely "further detail" about the story of creation. This makes the differences in the accounts only apparent rather than substantive. They are also insistent that this view of creation be taught as a scientific theory on par with the theory of evolution. They fight for what they call "scientific creationism." In their minds, it is as valid a scientific theory as any. They struggle forcefully to retain the teaching that Adam and Eve are literal, historical figures.

Another example is found in the tendency to weave biblical accounts into one seamless presentation. Thus, when the Synoptic Gospels (Matthew, Mark, Luke) describe Jesus' cleansing of the Temple as occurring at the end of Jesus' public ministry, and John positions it at the beginning of that ministry, fundamentalists view them as two separate occasions with one event taking place early on and the other later in Jesus' ministry (cf. Matt 21:12-13; Mark 11:15-17; Luke 19:45-46; John 2:13-17). Most scholars judge it highly unlikely that Jesus would have cleansed the Temple twice, given the volatile nature of that gesture. A more likely explanation is that the evangelists exercised poetic license in placing the story in separate locations in their Gospels for theological reasons rather than for historical ones.

The death of Judas provides another sample of how fundamentalists cope with biblical contradictions. One account narrates how Judas hanged himself in despair (Matt 27:5). A second account tells of Judas falling headlong and having his bowels burst open (Acts 1:18). Fundamentalists explain the discrepancy by coalescing the two accounts into one seamless story. They theorize that Judas hanged himself near a cliff, and the rope broke sending him tumbling down the cliff and bursting open. While this position is not inherently impossible, it seems a contorted way to explain what is more likely two separate traditions about the demise of the betrayer that circulated among different communities.

Most important in fundamentalist interpretation is that the Word of God cannot possibly be contradictory. One must look elsewhere for explanations of apparent contradictions. I should also note that not all fundamentalists are naive about the transmission of the biblical text. Some recognize that certain copies of the Greek New Testament or the Hebrew Bible could contain textual errors that crept in when an inattentive or less skilled scribe was copying from an earlier text. They maintain, however, that the autographs could not possibly have contained such mistakes.

Another aspect of hermeneutics concerns the fundamentalist claim that the meaning of passages in the Bible is self-evident. They claim that virtually anyone can pick up the Bible and understand it because its plain, literal sense is easily comprehensible. Yet the fact that *The Scofield Study Bible* itself is annotated and contains lengthy explanatory notes and interpretations tarnishes this assertion. Even fundamentalists need the assistance of knowledgeable outside experts to assist with biblical interpretation. Ancient literature, whether it is biblical or not, is not always easy to understand. Furthermore, since the Bible was written in foreign languages that few but experts know (Hebrew, Aramaic, Koine Greek), the average Christian is hampered in interpretation without the aid of tools and experts who can help explain the text.

Prophecy

The prophetic literature of the Bible is another area where fundamentalists have a distinct approach to interpretation. Since much of the Bible is prophecy and fulfillment, fundamentalists are intensely interested in how these prophecies are applicable today. Fundamentalists believe the Bible is directly intended for their use, today and in this modern context. Thus, prophecies are directed toward the present rather than the past. Little wonder that fundamentalists are attracted to the more dramatic prophetic books like Daniel or the book of Revelation. They believe that these books directly apply to modern times and describe the tremendous confrontation between good and evil, between God and Satan, that they believe is happening in the present. An example from a fundamentalist writer shows how narrow this perspective can be at times:

> Daniel's prophecy . . . was not a message to . . . Israel . . .
> nor was it a message to Judah! . . . The plain truth is, these
> prophecies were written for OUR PEOPLE OF OUR TIME,

and for no other previous people or time! They pertain to the world condition TODAY, and could not have been understood until today! . . . It is emphatically clear that these prophecies pertain to NO TIME but our time, in this Twentieth Century! (Quoted in Lloyd J. Averill, *Religious Right, Religious Wrong* [New York: Pilgrim Press, 1989] 133; emphases in the original).

The passage may be extreme in its perspective, but it illustrates well the fundamentalist tendency to interpret the Bible apart from its historical context. Direct and immediate application takes precedence over an interpretation rooted in history. As the third Christian millennium approached with the year 2000, some fundamentalists became obsessed with the idea that the second coming of Christ was imminent and that the prophecies of the Bible were finally coming to their climactic fulfillment. This attitude is not new in Christianity. Periodically in history, especially around significant dates such as the turn of a century or a millennium, groups have taken this same attitude. Some aspects of biblical prophecy lend themselves well to such fervor, such as the apocalyptic literature of the Bible (e.g., book of Daniel, Isa 24–27; Zech 9–14; Mark 13; Matt 24–25; book of Revelation). Characteristics of such apocalyptic literature coincide with the perspective of fundamentalists, including the following attitudes:

- a dualistic world view in which one is either right or wrong, there is no middle ground;
- the conviction that evil is more and more abounding in the world and conditions are getting worse;
- a deterministic belief that God has preordained the results of human history;
- a strong belief that a great cataclysmic confrontation between God and Satan will bring an end to human history and finally establish a righteous kingdom;
- an urgent call to all to lead a more ethically upright life in preparation for the victory of God over evil.

Since fundamentalists believe that prophecy directly applies to our time, there is less concern about what the passage might have meant when it was written rather than its applicability to our own day. In the late twentieth century, for instance, aspects of the book of Revelation were taken to refer to Russia and the collapse of communism. The gravitation toward such prophetic literature lends urgency to the fundamentalist message. It also reinforces the idea that they, like many prophets and saints before them, will have to suffer greatly to serve the cause of spreading the gospel message. Ultimately, they believe, they will be victorious and be part of the divine elect who enter the heavenly kingdom.

These are the major elements of the fundamentalist approach to the Bible. They concern the essential ideas of authority and canon, inspiration, hermeneutics, and prophecy. Naturally, interpretations of specific passages vary according to specific concerns, but the basic fundamentalist approach to biblical interpretation follows the principles and assumptions outlined above. We now turn to a brief exposition of a Catholic perspective on the Bible to see how it compares with the fundamentalist approach.

3

Bible Basics: A Catholic Approach to Scripture

How does a fundamentalist approach to the Bible compare with a Catholic approach? There is no one-to-one correspondence in approaches, yet all of the issues dealt with above can be treated in one way or another. After a few introductory comments, I will outline the main principles of a Catholic approach to Scripture.

Introductory comments

At the outset, one must recognize that the very organization of the Catholic Church is strikingly different from fundamentalist communities. Catholics have a hierarchical structure that guides the Church. Unlike fundamentalist communities, the Catholic Church has a set of official teachings about the Bible that is part of its magisterium (official body of Catholic teachings). These lay out clearly and succinctly the parameters of Catholic biblical interpretation. Moreover, because of the Catholic Church's esteem for the Bible, there exists an official department that is charged with oversight in the area of biblical studies. Pope Leo XIII founded the Pontifical Biblical Commission in 1902, consisting of an international team of experts on the Bible. Its purpose is to promote Catholic study of the Bible under the careful magisterial authority of the Holy See.

A second aspect of the Catholic perspective is the acceptance of modern, scientific methods of studying and interpreting the Bible. Catholics are not alone in embracing historical-critical and newer methods of studying the Bible. Most mainline Protestant denominations have a similar approach. The contrast, then, is not between Catholic and fundamentalist approaches to the Bible, but between those who accept scientific study of the Bible and those who do not. Unlike fundamentalists who view such biblical scholarship as undermining the Bible's authority, the Catholic Church has firmly embraced objective, scientific study of the Bible as essential. In essence, one of the targets of the fundamentalist battle against modernity is an accepted tool of the Catholic approach to Scripture.

A third introductory comment is a historical note. At one time Catholics, too, had what was essentially a fundamentalist approach to the Bible. Prior to the twentieth century the Catholic Church was as skeptical and fearful of scientific study of the Bible as many other Bible-toting Christians, even though the Bible did not figure as prominently in daily Catholic life as it did for Protestants. Two passages from Pope Leo XIII's encyclical on the Bible, *Providentissimus Deus* (1893), illustrate this point.

> For all the books which the Church receives as sacred and canonical are written wholly and entirely, with all their parts, at the dictation of the Holy Spirit; and so far is it from being possible that any error can coexist with inspiration, that inspiration not only is essentially incompatible with error, but excludes and rejects it as absolutely and necessarily as it is impossible that God Himself, the supreme Truth, can utter that which is not true.
>
> . . . It follows that those who maintain that error is possible in any genuine passage of the sacred writings either pervert the Catholic notion of inspiration or make God the author of such error (§§338, 340).

Note that the language is not that different from a typical fundamentalist position. Despite the enlightened nature of this encyclical, some ideas expressed in it were still caught up in a pre-scientific viewpoint. In the nineteenth century the

Church was not yet making the distinction in Scripture between lack of error in scientific and historical teaching and the lack of error in moral and religious truth.

Even into the early twentieth century the Catholic Church opposed some scientific studies that led to conclusions thought to be incompatible with Catholic teaching on the Bible. For example, the Church resisted for some time the conclusion of scholars that Moses himself could not have authored the first five books of the Old Testament (the Pentateuch), as ancient Jewish and Christian tradition held. To the contrary, there was strong evidence of multiple authors writing in different circumstances over a vast amount of time. For a time the Catholic Church rejected these new theories and held to the formal authorship of the Pentateuch by Moses. The Pontifical Biblical Commission attacked such scientific theories in a series of teachings between 1905 and 1915, which have subsequently been laid to rest.

We should note that despite some tendencies toward fundamentalism in its history, the Catholic Church has resisted using the terminology of "inerrancy" applied to the Bible. To the best of my knowledge, the word has never been used in official Church doctrine at the level of an ecumenical council. The word comes loaded with considerable baggage—a world view, we might say—that tilts toward an overly literal interpretation of the Bible. Vatican II uses the expression "without error" rather than the word "inerrancy" to avoid the innuendo of historical and scientific accuracy of the Bible (see *Dei Verbum,* the Constitution on Divine Revelation, #11; also quoted in the *Catechism of the Catholic Church,* §107). Although I will say more about this distinction below, we should note that the Catholic Church's position on lack of error in the Bible embraces only doctrinal and moral teaching, not scientific or historical. Furthermore, it allows for growth in the moral perspective in the Bible, recognizing that moral insight deepened over time. Not every moral teaching in the Bible carries the same weight.

In 1943, on the fiftieth anniversary of Leo XIII's encyclical, the Catholic Church's perspective on biblical interpretation changed dramatically. Pope Pius XII issued a groundbreaking

encyclical on biblical studies that gave Catholic biblical scholars the green light to employ all scientific means possible to explore the Bible in order to expound its meaning. A quotation
from this encyclical, *Divino Afflante Spiritu,* is instructive:

> Being thoroughly prepared by the knowledge of the ancient
> languages and by the aids afforded by the art of criticism, let
> the Catholic exegete undertake the task, of all those imposed
> on him the greatest, that, namely of discovering and expound-
> ing the genuine meaning of the Sacred Books. In the perfor-
> mance of this task let the interpreters bear in mind that their
> foremost and greatest endeavor should be to discern and de-
> fine clearly the sense of the biblical words which is called lit-
> eral. Aided by the context and by comparison with similar
> passages, let them therefore by means of their knowledge of
> languages search out with all diligence the literal meaning of
> the words . . . so that the mind of the author may be abun-
> dantly made clear (§23).

This position represented a shift from the encyclical of
Leo XIII. Not only did it provide the necessary impetus for
Catholic scholars to develop and exercise their skills to their
best ability, but it also exhorted Catholic exegetes to do their
work in freedom without fear of unjust harassment or ridicule.
While simultaneously acknowledging how few times the
Church has officially pronounced on the meaning of individual passages, one paragraph of Pius XII's encyclical calls
all Catholics to give honor and respect to the hard labor of
biblical scholars whose task is to explore the vast fund of
scriptural data for whatever profound meaning can be dis-
cerned. The Pope writes:

> There remain therefore many things, and of the greatest im-
> portance, in the discussion and exposition of which the skill
> and genius of Catholic commentators may and ought to be
> freely exercised, so that each may contribute his part to the
> advantage of all, to the continued progress of the sacred doc-
> trine and to the defense and honor of the Church (§47).

Ever since the issuance of this encyclical, Catholic scholars have been publicly engaged in scientific study of the
Bible. Many of the results of this scholarship influenced the

documents of Vatican II and continue to impact the post-conciliar life of the Church. Catholic biblical expertise, in a sense, came of age. Within a short span of time, Catholic biblical scholarship caught up with and equaled mainline Protestant biblical scholarship using the same scientific methods and tools, albeit interpreting from within the faith context of the Catholic Church. Names like Raymond E. Brown, S.S., Joseph A. Fitzmyer, S.J., and Roland E. Murphy, O.Carm., became internationally known as recognized experts on the Bible on par with their Protestant counterparts. Before them, some of their less famous predecessors had quietly made major advances in biblical studies behind the scenes, often researching the Bible in libraries and monasteries out of the public eye or only within the scholarly world. Their research helped lay the groundwork for Vatican II. Myriads of other Catholic scholars have followed their lead in scientific biblical study. This development has meant also that the Catholic approach to Scripture has not taken the path toward fundamentalism but toward the modern, critical study of the Bible which fundamentalism opposes.

A recent ecumenical statement effected between Southern Baptists and Roman Catholics offers a comparison of approaches to the Bible. On the one hand, the statement acknowledges the uniform respect of the Bible shared by the two faiths. Both use the Bible for spiritual instruction. Both also confess uniform faith in certain basic doctrines. The report nonetheless highlights ongoing differences:

> Southern Baptists and Roman Catholics believe in the triune God, the Father, the Son and the Holy Spirit, and we confess the full deity and perfect humanity of Jesus Christ. . . . On the basis of these core convictions, we addressed important issues where Roman Catholics and Southern Baptists have differed historically, including the inspiration and authority of the Bible, its inerrancy and infallibility, the role of the church in the interpretation of the Scriptures, and the nature and significance of historical-critical approaches to the study of the Bible ("Report on Sacred Scripture," *Origins* 29:17 [October 7, 1999] 266–67).

The report goes on to describe in brief detail these differences precisely in those areas we address in this book, e.g., revelation and the Word of God, inerrancy and infallibility of the Bible, historicity in the Bible, scientific study of the Bible, and the terminology of fundamentalism.

Milestones in Catholic teaching on the Bible

My final introductory comment offers some milestones in Catholic teaching on the Bible. These show the long tradition that has developed through the ages under the guidance of the Holy Spirit. Catholic teaching on the Bible has not been static. It has evolved over time, especially in the last two hundred years, into a sophisticated synthesis. I draw attention only to a few of the most important documents and their significance:

- Council of Trent, Fourth Session, 1546: This session finally settled any uncertainties about the canon of sacred Scripture that Catholics would use. The list of official books is what currently comprises the Catholic canon. This council also affirmed the priority of the Vulgate edition of the Bible (the Latin translation that began with St. Jerome) for official Catholic use.
- Vatican Council I, Constitution *Dei Filius,* 1870: This council affirmed the inspiration of the Bible and the fact that God is ultimately the author of the sacred Scriptures.
- *Providentissimus Deus,* Encyclical Letter of Pope Leo XIII, 1893: This nuanced encyclical presented a plan for Catholic scholars to study the Bible using some of the modern methods of biblical study that were emerging in the nineteenth century. It also warned, however, of the dangers of some scientific study and the possibility of being misled by false interpretations. It also fostered an unsophisticated understanding of "inerrancy," making no distinction between factual, historical issues in the Bible and religious or moral ones.
- Fourteen Decisions of the Pontifical Biblical Commission, 1905–1915: These decisions, in a sense, represent a step backward—but not totally. They were aimed at the excesses of interpretation that had accompanied some

"modernist" exploration of the Scriptures. The more conservative tone of these teachings led to the silencing of some important Catholic biblical scholars, such as the celebrated Dominican Marie-Joseph Lagrange, O.P., who founded the famous École Biblique in Jerusalem.

- *Spiritus Paraclitus,* Encyclical Letter of Pope Benedict XV, 1920: Issued on the fifteen hundredth anniversary of the death of St. Jerome, the great biblical scholar of the fourth–fifth centuries A.D., this rather conservative encyclical commended biblical scholars who were following the guidelines set down by Pope Leo XIII and using modern critical methods of study. It also warned against those who were underestimating the historical value of certain parts of Scripture.

- *Divino Afflante Spiritu,* Encyclical Letter of Pope Pius XII, 1943: This is the most important official document that inaugurated modern Catholic critical exegesis of the Bible. It affirms that the Bible contains no errors in faith and morals, but it also respects the human dimension of the Word of God. Catholic scholars are urged to concentrate on the literal meaning of Scripture while being sensitive to the many other deeper senses that expound its spiritual meaning.

- Instruction of the Pontifical Biblical Commission, "On the Historical Truth of the Gospels," 1964: This document is significant for its acknowledgment of the multi-layered traditions that are found in the canonical Gospels. It explains the threefold process by which the Gospels came into being: oral, written, and edited (redacted) traditions. Each of these corresponds to specific time frames: the time of Jesus and the apostles, the time of the preaching and collecting of traditions of later disciples, and the time of the evangelists who finally collected and edited the traditions for their individual communities. This process helps to explain why the literal meaning of the Gospels does not always represent "historical truth" as we might naively conceive of it. Careful discernment of the layers of the tradition and their theological intent is required to answer historical questions.

- Vatican Council II, *Dei Verbum*, Dogmatic Constitution on Divine Revelation, 1965: This is the most fundamental document because it is a dogmatic constitution of the Church formulated by an ecumenical council. Its extensive teaching affirms basic Catholic doctrine on the Bible, e.g., inspiration, lack of error in matters of faith and morals, the human dimension of the Scriptures that nonetheless communicates the divine message as God intended, and the fact that Scripture is "the soul of theology." It also notes the complex relationship of Scripture and Tradition as the fountains of divine revelation which give life to the Church, and it gives encouragement to Catholic biblical scholars for their important work.
- Instruction of the Pontifical Biblical Commission, "The Interpretation of the Bible in the Church," 1993: This is the most extensive official treatment of the many different modern methods of scientific biblical study that flourish in our day, both historical-critical methods and newer approaches. It reviews each of them, affirming what is positive and warning against what is negative in each method. Only fundamentalism is sharply criticized as incompatible with a Catholic approach to Scripture.
- *Catechism of the Catholic Church*, §§101–41, 1997 (2nd ed.): This resource, of course, is the most convenient and succinct summary of the Church's teaching on the Bible. It frequently quotes earlier documents from Vatican II, papal encyclicals, and pronouncements of the Pontifical Biblical Commission, as well as older resources (e.g., the Fathers of the Church).

Even though this list of milestones does not do justice to the extent and the nuances of the Church's teaching on the Bible, one can see that it is a development of a tradition. The Church has not taken a monolithic view of how one is to approach sacred Scripture for discerning God's will. The Catholic position has progressed from what was essentially a pre-critical and ahistorical view of the Bible, consistent with fundamentalism, to a highly nuanced and historically-conscious view that stands in opposition to a fundamentalist approach.

Principles of Catholic interpretation of the Bible

Drawing upon various magisterial teachings of the Catholic Church, especially as presented in the *Catechism of the Catholic Church* (2nd ed. [Vatican City: Libreria Editrice Vaticana, 1997]), I will summarize the main characteristics of a Catholic approach to Scripture.

(1) Very basic to a Catholic approach to Scripture is the acceptance of two interrelated sources of knowing God's will, Scripture and Tradition. At the very outset, then, Catholics have a basic stance that opposes the fundamentalist idea of *sola scriptura*. To quote Vatican II's Dogmatic Constitution on Divine Revelation:

> The Church has always venerated the divine Scriptures as she venerated the Body of the Lord . . . to offer it to the faithful from the one table of the Word of God and the Body of Christ. She has always regarded, and continues to regard, the Scriptures, taken together with sacred Tradition, as the supreme rule of her faith (*Dei Verbum* §21, quoted from Austin Flannery, ed., *Vatican Council II: The Conciliar and Post Conciliar Documents* [Collegeville: The Liturgical Press, 1975] 762).

This quotation shows the essential connection between the Bible, as God's holy Word, and the magisterial Tradition of the Church. From a Catholic perspective, as important as the Bible is, it cannot serve alone as the sole source of revelation. We should note, however, that the word "Tradition" (note the capital "T") does not mean "traditions" we remember as we grew up. Rather, it refers to the Church's magisterial teaching through the ages as it has interpreted the Scriptures, interacted with them, and formulated doctrines that expound God's revelation as humans can know it. We should also mention that Vatican II's position does not precisely define the complex interrelationship between Scripture and Tradition. They are not opposites, nor are they two entirely distinct sources. Instead, they are intertwined with one another yet distinctive enough to sustain separate identities. They constitute one "sacred deposit" of revelation yet with individual identities. The Catholic position implicitly acknowledges that not every teaching of the Church can be found in sacred Scripture. The Holy Spirit continues to guide the Church to understand God's revelation as it evolves and is revealed through the ages. The Scriptures will always play a crucial role in this process, but they are not the sole authority for our faith. The Church's living magisterial office is charged with ultimately determining the meaning of Scripture where necessary, under the guidance of the Holy Spirit.

(2) The Catholic Church also recognizes a type of "inerrancy" of the Bible, but only in faith and morals, not in science and history. Yet Catholicism shuns using the actual word "inerrancy" because of the strong connotation of literalist interpretation that it embodies. A quotation from the Constitution on Divine Revelation illustrates the Catholic position.

> Since, therefore, all that the inspired authors, or sacred writers, affirm should be regarded as affirmed by the Holy Spirit, we must acknowledge that the books of Scripture, firmly, faithfully and without error, teach that truth which God, for the sake of our salvation, wished to see confided to the sacred Scriptures (*Dei Verbum* §11).

This assertion of a lack of error, which affirms the understanding that sacred Scripture is inspired by God, is coupled with the charge to interpret the Scriptures carefully through the exploration of their expression:

> Seeing that, in sacred Scripture, God speaks through men [sic] in human fashion, it follows that the interpreter of sacred Scripture, if he is to ascertain what God has wished to communicate to us, should carefully search out the meaning which the sacred writers really had in mind, that meaning which God had thought well to manifest through the medium of their words (*Dei Verbum* §12).

Implicit in this stance is the recognition that interpreters must honor the various literary forms found in the Bible. The biblical authors employed many different forms (narratives, poems, hymns, laws, parables, miracle stories, proverbs, sayings, apocalyptic visions, etc.) that require careful discernment to arrive at a proper understanding of their meaning.

The medium does affect the message. Another practical import of Vatican II's position is that a Catholic interpretation of a passage of Scripture is not bothered by inconsistencies or inaccuracies that some of the ancient writings contain. Human errors of a scientific or historical nature are not unexpected in ancient literature, and the Bible is no exception. Let's take a few examples.

The Catholic position on the creation stories of Genesis is not to take them literally in every detail. In fact, Pope John Paul II has indicated clearly that the scientific theory of evolution is not necessarily incompatible with the Genesis stories of creation. We recognize that the stories of Genesis 1–11 are couched in mythological language that was quite consistent with the perspective of many ancient Near Eastern cultures of the tenth–ninth centuries B.C. when the stories were likely composed. This is not an assertion that the scientific theory of evolution is absolutely correct. It remains a theory, but not one that contradicts the biblical accounts. Instead, the biblical accounts are recognized as a non-scientific scenario of creation whose primary purpose is to affirm that God ultimately ordered creation and that it is good. Thus Adam and Eve need not be literal, historical individuals but representative figures of the first human beings. Catholic teaching only insists that at some point God placed within humankind a soul that distinguishes people from all other beings, something that need not contradict a theory of evolution.

Another example comes from the New Testament. Catholics teach that the Gospels consist of three stages of tradition about Jesus that grew over time. These are (a) the actual life and teaching of Jesus, (b) the oral traditions rooted in the preaching of the first disciples, and (c) the written traditions that were collected and edited into the Gospels as we know them. (See *Catechism of the Catholic Church,* §126.) Acknowledging this process allows one to cope with possible contradictory passages, multiple versions of the same basic story, accretions to the details as stories were told and retold over decades, and the like. There is no need to reconcile every apparent contradiction or to merge into one seamless story the details of Jesus' birth, life, ministry, death, and resurrection.

Catholics recognize the Gospels as a collection of oral, written, and edited traditions that developed in diverse contexts in the early decades of the Christian community. Thus they can contain diverse perspectives that are not always reconcilable with one another. As they exist now, they are not eyewitness accounts of Jesus' ministry but theological presentations of the stories of Jesus of Nazareth.

(3) A Catholic approach to the Bible accepts the necessity to read the text in a literal fashion, but it also goes beyond that. Reading the Bible literally, i.e., what the words mean in their plain sense, is one thing. Reading literalistically, in which one slavishly interprets each word in a narrow fashion, is something else. Whereas fundamentalists read many passages literalistically, Catholics recognize a deeper sense in Scripture that can go beyond the literal meaning of the words. This has been called in recent times the *sensus plenior* (Latin, "deeper sense"). Traditionally, the Catholic Church has also remained open to what is known as the "spiritual sense" of sacred Scripture, which at times can be equated with the deeper sense. The *Catechism of the Catholic Church* once more summarizes Catholic tradition. It calls attention to the traditional way of subdividing the deeper, more spiritual interpretation of Scripture into three sub-categories: the allegorical, the moral, and the anagogical senses (§117).

The allegorical sense recognizes that the Scriptures sometimes present "typologies" or extensive allegories in which there is meant to be a one-to-one correspondence between an image used and its deeper meaning. Thus, an Old Testament image like the Exodus from Egypt can represent Christian baptism (e.g., 1 Cor 10:2), or seemingly common images like blood and water can take on the sacramental significance of Eucharist and baptism (e.g., John 19:34). The moral sense refers to the general ability of many Scriptures to give ethical instruction (e.g., the Sermon on the Mount, Matthew 5–7). Finally, the anagogical sense (from Greek, *anagō*, "lead") refers to the deeper understanding that all of the sacred Scriptures are intended to lead us to the kingdom of God, and they therefore have instructional value as we journey toward the "heavenly Jerusalem" (Rev 21:1–22:5).

Each of these deeper senses grows out of and is based upon the literal sense. They cannot contradict the literal sense of the writings, but neither is their meaning limited to it. The senses also overlap at times. Historically, the early Fathers of the Church exercised these interpretational methods quite freely. Then and especially during the Middle Ages, some of these approaches led to bizarre and exaggerated interpretations. The Church warns that this is always a danger when one allows for deeper interpretations that go beyond the surface meaning (see *Interpretation in the Life of the Church*, III). Yet allowance for a multiplicity of meanings preserves the eternal value of the Word of God and its applicability for many different generations.

To be complete, I should emphasize that a Catholic approach does not assume that all interpretations are equal in value. Any interpreter can purposefully or accidentally read into a text something that is not there. This is called "eisegesis." It contrasts with "exegesis," which is the task of interpreting *from* Scripture. While the deeper sense can never be fully mined for all that it might be, interpreters are not free simply to imagine any meaning they wish beyond the literal sense. Not only are there boundaries to what words can mean, but the Church bears ultimate responsibility for delimiting fantastic interpretations that are not consistent with its teaching.

(4) Catholics also recognize the canonicity of the Bible. Indeed, the Catholic canon is defined as forty-six books in the Old Testament and twenty-seven in the New. (For a historical reason, the Protestant canon has a smaller set of thirty-nine Old Testament books. See Witherup, *The Bible Companion*, 12–15.) Unlike fundamentalists, however, Catholics emphasize that the origin of the canon lies in a formal decision by the early Church to declare certain books canonical, inspired literature and to exclude other books from the list. In a sense, the process was bidirectional. From one direction, the Scriptures helped to form the community of the Church, but from another direction, the Church, under the guidance of the Holy Spirit, finally made the decision about what books to include in the official canonical collection. Someone had to organize and proclaim the limits of the

canon; it did not appear independently of the Christian community by divine fiat. Some of the New Testament writings (e.g., Paul's letters) circulated in collected fashion around the early Christian communities before the Church ever formally declared canonical literature. In the case of the Old Testament writings, which were for the early Church the primary sacred writings, the canon probably existed by around A.D. 90. For the New Testament the process of setting the canon certainly concluded by the time of St. Athanasius (ca. A.D. 367), but it had already begun to be formulated as early as A.D. 90. Most importantly, we should note that the Scriptures did not grow independently of the Christian community itself but in tandem with it.

(5) The Catholic Church strongly accepts the doctrine of inspiration in relation to the Scriptures, but it does not adhere to any one theory of inspiration. There have been multiple attempts throughout the history of theology to formulate a theory that explains how inspiration works. A Catholic approach no longer accepts a simplistic dictation theory, but at the same time it affirms the role of the Holy Spirit in inspiring the human author to write the Word of God in order to communicate faithfully God's will. In place of any specific theory of inspiration, the Catholic Church offers three guiding hermeneutical principles for interpretation of Scripture in accordance with the Holy Spirit who inspired it. These are summarized succinctly in the *Catechism*.

(A) Be especially attentive "to the content and unity of the whole of Scripture."
(B) Read the Scripture within "the living Tradition of the whole Church."
(C) Be attentive to the analogy of faith. (i.e., the coherence of all the truths of faith within the plan of divine Revelation) (*Catechism of the Catholic Church*, §§ 112–14).

The effect of these three principles is to broaden the context of interpretation. It includes the contexts of the canon as a whole and the Church's teaching through the ages. The word *context*, in fact, is vitally important. From a Catholic perspective, the Scriptures should not be read outside the larger context of the Church's Tradition and the entire biblical canon itself. The late eminent Catholic biblical scholar, Sulpician Father Raymond E. Brown, used to tell his lecture audiences, "A passage is biblical only when it is *in the Bible*." In other words, interpreting passages by considering them individually and removing them from their context within the Bible can (and often does) lead to misinterpretation. Taking seriously the need to keep in perspective the whole of the biblical canon, while one is simultaneously trying to understand a single passage, requires discipline and an openness to history. Let's take an example from the prophetic literature.

We will look briefly at three distinct passages from the Old Testament, from the books of Isaiah, Micah, and Joel. Two of them are identical and seemingly speak of a pacificist image, but the third one apparently reverses the image and thus changes the interpretation:

> He shall judge between the nations, / and shall arbitrate for many peoples; / they shall beat their *swords into plowshares*, / and their *spears into pruning hooks;* / nation shall not lift up sword against nation, / neither shall they learn war any more (Isa 2:4).

> He shall judge between many peoples, / and shall arbitrate between strong nations far away; / they shall beat their *swords into plowshares*, / and their *spears into pruning hooks;* / nation shall not lift up sword against nation, / neither shall they learn war any more . . . (Mic 4:3).

> Beat your *plowshares into swords*, / and your *pruning hooks into spears;* / let the weakling say, "I am a warrior" (Joel 3:10).

Taken out of context, the highlighted words from Joel are in direct contrast to those from Isaiah and Micah. The first two passages date from the eighth century B.C., the time of two great prophets, Isaiah and Micah. The passages are so verbally similar that most scholars believe one is dependent upon the other, though it is impossible to say definitively who copied from whom. In the historical context of that time, each prophet is addressing the issue of the threat that their powerful northern neighbor Assyria posed to the fledgling country of Israel. Each of these two prophets received God's Word in his own way and passed it on to his contemporaries to urge their steadfast faith and confidence in God. The prophets basically preached reliance only on God and not on any conventional political maneuvering. One day God would make an end to warfare and bring all the nations together in peace and harmony. They would need no reliance upon the strategies of warfare for peace and security.

At a later time (sometime after the exile, perhaps in the sixth century B.C.) the prophet Joel was addressing an entirely different situation. His words are part of a vision of the reckoning that will come upon all nations on the eschatological judgment day when God has promised to set all things right. Through the prophet God calls them to arms, but for the purposes of judgment "on that day," i.e., the day of God's just reckoning. The peaceful vision of Isaiah and Micah offered two centuries earlier is reversed and made into a call for war, albeit a war in which God will be the final victor and judge. These passages are not meant broadly to give opposing advice in any circumstance. Instead, each applied specifically to certain situations which God addressed by specific prophecies in different contexts. Without the historical and literary contexts, there is no way of understanding accurately how these biblical messages reveal God's intentions. The prophets do, in fact, offer different advice. That is because God's Word came to them in different circumstances. The differing messages do not thereby compromise the truth of the Scriptures, but place them appropriately in their own proper contexts for future generations to explore.

The real hermeneutical challenge, of course, is to apply biblical passages to contemporary situations in ways that are faithful to the text. The words of Isaiah and Micah more likely appeal to our Christian sensibilities today, but the words of Joel stand in the biblical canon as a witness to another perspective in other circumstances.

In summary, while Catholics and fundamentalists have some elements in common, they part ways on most interpretive methods and issues of the Bible. Let me summarize the contrast by means of a convenient chart:

Fundamentalist Perspective on the Bible	Catholic Perspective on the Bible
The Bible *is* the Word of God	The Bible is God's Word in human words
Scripture *alone*	Scripture *and* Tradition
Emphasis on literalist reading of Bible	Emphasis on literal (not literalist) reading as well as deeper (and spiritual) meanings
Tendency to view inspiration narrowly	Tendency to take a broad view of inspiration
Inerrancy of the Bible in all matters	No errors in the Bible only on matters of faith and morals
Lack of historical perspective in interpretation	Historical perspective is essential for interpretation
Frequent interpretations out of context	Necessity of interpretations in context, especially the context of the sacred canon
Direct and immediate applicability of most biblical passages	Mostly indirect applicability of biblical passages
Denial of role of Church in canonization of Scripture	Recognition of role of Church in canonization process
Tendency to ignore history of interpretation	History of interpretation essential
Narrow and precise prophetic eschatology often linked to a time line	Broad and imprecise eschatology not linked to any specific time line
Rejection of scientific historical-critical methods of interpretation	Acceptance of scientific historical-critical methods of interpretation (among others)

Many of these differences show up in specific interpretations, but even some of the general principles are divergent. Most important is the Catholic acceptance of modern critical studies of the Bible and the respect for the literary and historical context of each and every passage of the Bible. The Church seldom defines the meaning of specific passages but gives general guidance to reading the Scriptures within the larger context of the Catholic faith.

4

An Evaluation of Biblical Fundamentalism

Now that we have laid out the alternate approaches of fundamentalism and Catholicism to the Bible, we are in a better position to evaluate the strengths and weaknesses of fundamentalism. As I warned in the introduction, we should try to make a judgment that is both fair and as objective as possible. We will begin by first analyzing why fundamentalism is, in fact, attractive to many people today.

Why is biblical fundamentalism attractive?

Accurate numbers are not readily available to confirm the influence of biblical fundamentalism. Sociologists indicate that it is somewhat on the wane. Interestingly, in October 2000 former President Jimmy Carter publicly announced his departure from the Southern Baptist Convention because of overly rigid doctrines. In particular, he singled out the inability to carry on a respectful dialogue with those in disagreement, fundamentalist restrictions on the role of women in church and society, and an overly literal interpretation of Scripture. This action is symbolic of the struggle that has been taking place in the Southern Baptist Convention for some years between the more fundamentalist wing and the more moderate wing. Yet fundamentalist communities seem to be flourishing in various parts of the world, notably in Africa and South America, and the political discussions that make the headlines in the U.S. indicate that fundamentalists still have considerable influence in conservative circles. The fact is that fundamentalism offers some attraction. Many people, Catholics included, become interested in a fundamentalist approach to Scripture for a variety of reasons, including psychological, social, and religious.

(1) One attraction of biblical fundamentalism is *the Bible itself*. Fundamentalists' devotion to the Bible is admirable. It is akin to the attraction that some pagans in the ancient world felt when they observed the Jews who were devoted to their sacred writings. They became known as "the people of the book." The fact that fundamentalists read the Bible daily, memorize many passages, study it in some depth, and share thoughts about it with one another can be fascinating for those who feel that their own faith communities do not nourish this aspect of faith. I have known many Catholics who have, by default, attended fundamentalist Bible study groups because it was the only alternative.

Although many Catholics thirst for Bible knowledge, they do not always find organized Bible study readily at hand. (From another perspective, pastors are sometimes frustrated when they offer adult Bible sessions and find that few Catholics come!) Many Catholic parishes, in particular, have few opportunities for formal Bible study. Unlike most Protestant churches, the Catholic Church has not successfully gotten its members in the habit of reading and praying the Bible daily. Catholics are certainly encouraged to read and pray the Bible, especially by preparing the lectionary readings at Mass in advance. But the fact is that using the Bible is not yet a daily regimen for many Catholics.

(2) Another attraction is that the fundamentalist approach to faith offers a *personal* side of faith that is often lacking in Catholicism. People can identify with the idea of Jesus being their personal Lord and Savior. The thought that God's love for an individual is so strong that God would send his own Son to be a Savior is very consoling in a world where indi-

viduals can feel lost and neglected. The notion that Jesus Christ died for *me* is quite profound. It comforts and strengthens. Yet Catholic faith, in particular, has emphasized the communal dimension of salvation to such a degree that the personal side can get lost. The demand to make a personal decision for Jesus can be an attractive challenge to someone who is seeking to deepen his or her faith.

Moreover, from a sociological perspective, the fundamentalist emphasis on individual faith dovetails well with the American predilection for individualism. Not only does it emphasize personal responsibility, but it also gives an individual a greater sense of control and freedom. A personal decision to follow Jesus, to assent to the gospel message, and to live an ethically upright life gives one a sense of purpose and fulfillment.

This personal dimension can be frightening for some Catholics. Sometimes, Catholics have asked me how to respond to the fundamentalist question, "Do you believe Jesus Christ is your personal Lord and Savior?" My response is simple. Of course, we Catholics can assent to that question affirmatively. Jesus Christ is our personal Lord and Savior, too. But this formulaic statement is not an end in itself. We go beyond that to add that salvation is intended for a community and not for individuals alone. Jesus gathered a group of disciples around him and taught them to pray together. He did not simply call them individually. They were to form the nucleus of a new community, a community of disciples. We believe that the Church is an essential part of that faith to which Jesus calls us, but we do not thereby reject the personal challenge that comes with that faith. We try to put it in its proper communal context.

Another aspect of this personal dimension of Catholic faith that can easily be overlooked is in our celebration of the sacrament of confirmation. In the decades following Vatican II the sacrament of confirmation has been the topic of much discussion. It has more recently emphasized the need for a personal commitment to faith at some point in a person's life. Baptism as an infant does not make one a good member of the Church if that initial commitment is not strengthened, nourished, and molded by a personal, adult commitment. When we as young adults have our faith sealed in the Holy Spirit, we are being asked to take responsibility for our faith. Jesus is calling us, and we are asked to respond. There is a strong personal dimension to Catholic faith, but it sometimes gets lost amid other factors.

(3) A third attraction to fundamentalism is the emphasis on the *direct and unmediated experience of God* by means of faith. This is also appealing in a society where individualism and freedom are emphasized. In a sense, fundamentalists promote a highly privatized religion. To think that we need no outside authority to receive God's will empowers individuals tremendously. Fundamentalism promotes a "God-and-me" or "Jesus-and-me" type of religion. If only I open the Bible, God will speak directly to me in clear and unmistakable terms. This individualistic approach also feeds our modern anti-institutional biases. Who needs a church or priests or outside experts if the Word of God is available freely for the taking? Group Bible study can also feed into this perspective. The fundamentalist approach emphasizes that the Scriptures are meant for *me*. What a passage means to *me* at this particular time in my life is uppermost in discerning God's will. The promise of what is essentially a direct line to God's intentions for one's own life is attractive.

(4) For many people a major attraction to fundamentalism is primarily psychological. It offers *security and certainty* in a world that is increasingly insecure and uncertain. From an internal perspective, fundamentalism is a neatly tied together package of questions and answers. It can offer psychological comfort to those unable or unwilling to cope with life's uncertainties, ambiguities, and the multiple choices that must be made day after day. When one buys into the fundamentalist approach, one receives a comprehensive world view that says, "Don't worry, God is in charge. Things may appear to be degenerating—especially morally, but God will set it all right." No one can deny the fast pace of modern life and the effect it has had on our very consumer-oriented society. Life is hectic and confusing, and change is occurring at an increasingly rapid rate. The number of ethical questions

that have emerged in the medical field alone is staggering. Issues of genetic engineering, cloning, managing both the conception and termination of life, health care, and so on are developing at such a rate that it seems impossible to keep up. Where does one get a sense of calm and inner direction in a world that so dramatically evolves day to day? Where does one find a steady compass to guide one through the stormy seas of the fast-paced and confusing alternatives of modern life?

When one adds all the other areas where ethical issues arise (family life, marriage and divorce, business practices, the use of the internet, nuclear energy, the arms race, capital punishment, the spread of communicable diseases, etc.) the effect can be overwhelming. A system whereby certain basic principles govern all decisions, such as life and death issues, offers an attractive alternative to the helter-skelter growth of options in modern life. Fundamentalism is also attractive because it avoids the complexity and ambiguity of many modern questions. A life lived in either/or choices is more comfortable than one that requires learning all the intricacies of an issue in order to make an informed decision. Gray areas are quagmires of uncertainty to be avoided. Fundamentalism helps people avoid ambiguity. It sets clear boundaries and goals, and as such, helps people cope with modern life.

(5) There is also a *sociological reason* for the attractiveness of fundamentalism. Sociologists point to the phenomenon of strong groups and weak groups in society. One likely reason for the strong appeal of fundamentalism in a complex, changing world is that it exhibits characteristics of a "strong" group. One scholar has summarized these characteristics under six headings: (a) strong commitment; (b) discipline; (c) missionary zeal; (d) absolutism; (e) conformity to a set ideology; and (f) fanaticism. (See Dean M. Kelley, *Why Conservative Churches Are Growing* [New York: Harper & Row, 1972].) These indicators of a strong group stand in direct opposition to "weak" groups which exhibit relativism, diversity, dialogue, indecisiveness, individualism, and the lack of desire to have one's ideas exposed to others.

In a society that emphasizes the characteristics of weak groups fundamentalism has obvious appeal. Its stance is essentially counter-cultural, something that reinforces both its identity and its tendency to separate itself from the mainstream. It is worth noting that this sociological phenomenon of religious zealots separating themselves from the dominant culture appears throughout the history of Judeo-Christian religion. Even in Jesus' day certain Jews exhibited such tendencies (e.g., the Essenes who took themselves to the Dead Sea to preserve their understanding of authentic Jewish faith) that can be seen, at least in part, as fundamentalist in orientation.

(6) Yet another attraction is the *sense of community* that exists among many fundamentalist groups. As compared to many large mainline Protestant churches and Catholic parishes, fundamentalist groups emphasize the importance of supporting one another in community. They truly work at promoting a sense of belonging to a caring group of people in imitation of the early Church as it is ideally described in the Acts of the Apostles (e.g., Acts 2:43-47). This attraction does not contradict the emphasis on the personal dimension of faith but complements it.

On several occasions I have personally witnessed the strong sense of support fundamentalists can offer. In one circumstance I saw how strongly a fundamentalist community came to the aid of a member and her family when it was discovered that she had terminal cancer. The incredible support they offered her, materially and spiritually, was truly exemplary. In another instance, in a very rural island community off the coast of Alaska, the local Assembly of God minister and his tiny community were the main force in offering hospitality to all the professional fishermen who happened to pass by. He and his family offered them food, shelter, counseling, or whatever they might need from the family's own limited resources. His was the only functioning social outreach on the island, despite the presence of other Christians.

Fellowship is an important value among fundamentalists. In a world where many people feel lonely and unappreciated, belonging to a community that takes an interest in and cares for its individual members is certainly attractive. This is not say that other church communities do not offer hospitality and fellowship, but they are a hallmark of many fundamentalist communities.

These six reasons explain, at least in part, why some people find fundamentalism appealing. How does a Catholic evaluate such a system?

Are there positive aspects to biblical fundamentalism?

There are some positive aspects that come not from the system of biblical fundamentalism itself, but from its adherents. These flow directly from the reasons that it attracts followers.

(1) The fundamentalists' professed *respect for the Bible* as God's Word and their willingness to engage it for Christian living is admirable. The fact that other Christians, Catholics among them, would not approach the Bible the same way does not negate their good intentions. They attempt to take the Bible seriously and put it to use. It is not merely a history book for them, nor is it just an antiquated word from the past. They seek to encounter God's Word as a living, breathing Word that can direct their lives.

(2) A second positive aspect is the *personal dimension of faith* that characterizes fundamentalist communities. They take seriously the gospel challenge to make faith a personal decision. They stand by this commitment and they work hard at deepening it on a regular basis, especially through studying the Bible. The evangelistic urge and zeal that accompany this personal decision can also be admirable. One can question whether it is really wise to get on a soapbox at a street corner and loudly proclaim a religious message while the rest of the world goes blithely by, but one has to admire the personal testimony to faith that fundamentalists profess.

(3) Fundamentalists are also positively committed to promoting *good, healthy family life.* Along with many others in society, fundamentalists believe that modern American culture is tearing the traditional family apart. Divorce and remarriage are widespread. The inability to make a permanent commitment of any kind undermines stability in marriage and family life. In fact, the very definition of a married relationship is under attack. Family life is often so busy, with both parents working at

trying to make a living, that children are sometimes neglected. Like Mormons and some other groups, biblical fundamentalists take seriously the need to promote family life. They schedule activities with the family in mind. An unfortunate downside to this aspect is the concomitant emphasis on stereotypical roles of men and women in the family. Fundamentalists favor some parts of the New Testament that limit the roles of women in society (e.g., Eph 5:22-33). They apply the roles of husband and wife mechanically, frowning upon women working outside the home. Promoting values of marriage and family is good, but canonizing certain social models in the Bible, taken out of their historical context, as normative for all time is a practice non-fundamentalists would prefer to avoid.

(4) Fundamentalism's emphasis on *personal moral responsibility* is also admirable. In an age that often promotes "passing the buck" of responsibility to others, or generically to society, fundamentalists call people to personal accountability. Maintaining a personal moral code forces one to live up to an external standard of behavior that challenges people beyond their own self-interest.

(5) The fundamentalist emphasis on *fundamentals* has a positive aspect to it. There may be a human tendency to desire short-hand, concise summary statements of values that promote identity and distinctiveness. Regardless of the reason, the penchant to focus on certain essentials in life that should not be compromised is a good impulse. The Church, in fact, has done that through the ages with formulations of creeds in different eras, formulaic oaths, collections of beliefs in catechisms, etc. Catholics, too, would assent to certain fundamentals of the faith that are indisputable. The challenge is to uphold certain fundamentals without becoming fundamentalist.

(6) Fundamentalists' *strong sense of community* is another plus. Their idealization of the Christian community in the New Testament may be exaggerated, but they are correct in emphasizing the need for solid and supportive communities of faith. Fundamentalists are not alone in this value, but it is a priority that they take seriously. It also helps to provide some balance to their highly personalized dimension of faith.

What are the weaknesses of fundamentalism?

Despite some positive dimensions to the way fundamentalists live their lives, a Catholic perspective sees serious weaknesses in biblical fundamentalism. It is essentially incompatible with Catholic faith. In fact, in an important document issued to commemorate the one-hundredth anniversary of Leo XIII's encyclical on the Bible, the Pontifical Biblical Commission explained clearly the dangers of biblical fundamentalism. The Commission's document, which is otherwise quite positive on the value of the large variety of contemporary approaches to the Bible, reserves its strongest negative judgment for fundamentalism:

> The fundamentalist approach is dangerous, for it is attractive to people who look to the Bible for ready answers to the problems of life. It can deceive these people, offering them interpretations that are pious but illusory, instead of telling them that the Bible does not contain an immediate answer to each and every problem. Without saying as much in so many words, fundamentalism actually invites people to a kind of intellectual suicide. It injects into life a false certitude, for it unwittingly confuses the divine substance of the biblical message with what are in fact its human limitations (*The Interpretation of the Bible in the Church* [Rome: Pontifical Biblical Commission, 1993] §I.F).

The Commission points out fundamentalism's overly simplistic approach to life and the Bible's application to it. Cardinal Joseph Ratzinger, head of the Vatican's Congregation for the Doctrine of the Faith, also commented on this deficiency in fundamentalism in a conference on biblical studies in the late 1980s:

> Fundamentalism is a danger. That is clear. It is absolutely incompatible with the Catholic faith, because the Catholic faith supposes that I read the Bible in the context of the community of faith and the community of all the centuries of faith. Thus I read the Bible with the church and with the faith of all times. And I read it reasonably, in a reasonable manner. So we must strive to avoid fundamentalism (quoted in Richard

John Neuhaus, *Biblical Interpretation in Crisis* [Grand Rapids, Mich.: Eerdmans, 1989] 140).

This dual problem of reading the Bible simplistically and out of context is the major weakness in fundamentalism. There is a natural human tendency to want simple answers, but modern life does not always lend itself to simple solutions to the complex problems that have evolved over time. The one-to-one correspondence between a modern problem and the Bible's application to it breaks down very quickly. That is why fundamentalism is unacceptable. But more can be said about fundamentalism's limitations. In addition to its overly simplistic approach, I point out eight weaknesses.

(1) Most obvious is fundamentalism's *lack of historical perspective*. Fundamentalists have a very narrow view of human history. Indeed, they are almost ahistorical when it comes to the origins of the Bible. The Bible is viewed as a pristine document that was revealed in a singular divine act that is valid for all time. Passages are routinely interpreted out of context with little regard to their historical origins. Fundamentalists have difficulties with the real or apparent contradictions in the Bible precisely because of their lack of historical consciousness. They acknowledge no opportunity for a development of perspective, especially in the area of moral teaching in the Bible. Most principles are read as if they were written specifically for modern times. (They would acknowledge some exceptions, e.g., the food laws of the book of Leviticus.) The "now" perspective overshadows any sense of history.

(2) Fundamentalism also has a *limited view of revelation*. Since they view the Bible as the final word on just about any topic, there is no room for the development of doctrine over time or for reformulations of Christian doctrine in history, as other churches acknowledge. Even the basic creeds accepted by mainline Christian churches, such as the Apostles' Creed or the Nicene Creed, are not deemed important by fundamentalists. The Word of God alone, as expounded by fundamentalist interpreters, is what is essential.

(3) Another serious limitation is ironically fundamentalism's *a-biblical perspective*. Fundamentalism purports to

rely solely on the Bible and its self-evident message for its foundations, but the reality is otherwise. A glance at *The New Scofield Study Bible,* for instance, reveals that many insights contained in the footnotes are actually formulations of doctrines that are outside the Bible and imposed upon it. Such is the case with "dispensationalism" which this Bible edition popularized. The teaching of the seven "dispensations" is an artificial construction of salvation history comparable to many other doctrinal schemas in history. This theory divides the history of the world into seven covenants or dispensations, each based on a specific biblical passage, through which God's relation to humanity has been enacted. The seven are:

- The Dispensation of Innocence (Gen 1:28; the Garden of Eden)
- The Dispensation of Conscience or Moral Responsibility (Gen 3:7; from the Fall of Adam and Eve to Noah)
- The Dispensation of Human Government (Gen 8:15; from Noah to the covenant with Abraham)
- The Dispensation of Promise (Gen 12:1; from the patriarch Abraham to Moses)
- The Dispensation of Law (Exod 19:1; from Moses the lawgiver to Jesus Christ)
- The Dispensation of Church (Acts 2:1; from the death and resurrection of Jesus Christ to the present)
- The Dispensation of Kingdom (Rev 20:4; begins when Christ returns to earth in victory)

According to this theory, in each of the six dispensations humanity failed to live up to God's expectations. Each time God placed humanity under certain expectations, but because human stewardship of these commands failed, God will finally act in the last dispensation with the kingdom established by Jesus Christ who will finally defeat evil and establish the thousand-year reign of peace. The schema is a systematic interpretation of Scripture, but it remains just that—an interpretation based upon a schema that is artificial and randomly chooses certain key passages as its main pillars. Ironically, fundamentalism's belief in dispensationalism also leads to a minimalization of the four Gospels in comparison to other parts of the New Testament (i.e., Paul's letters, the book of Revelation). Fundamentalism's honoring of the place of the Bible in Christian life actually conceals the true intention to create a unified system that tries to formulate simple answers to life's questions. The Bible provides a convenient tool, but it is paradoxically used to prop up a system that is extrinsic to the Bible itself. This is a serious inconsistency in fundamentalism.

(4) Fundamentalism also creates a *"canon within a canon,"* thus limiting the Bible to a series of crucial passages that undergird the fundamentalist system while ignoring other passages that might challenge its assumptions. This is apparent in the approach to biblical prophecy. The prophetic literature of the Bible is far more important than the wisdom literature. There is a narrow perspective on prophecy that reduces it to prediction and fulfillment, with little regard for the historical grounding of the prophetic word. Prophets in the Old Testament had in view their own people in their own time and in the near future, not the distant future, and certainly not more than two thousand years later. The applicability of the prophetic word depends on understanding it in its historical context first, before trying to apply it to today.

Also, fundamentalists have essential passages (usually in the *Authorized King James Version*) that are referred to over and over again and central to their belief. John 3:16 ("For God so loved the world . . ."), Romans 10:9 ("if thou shalt confess with thy mouth the Lord Jesus . . ."), John 3:3 ("Except a man be born again . . .") are quoted again and again without regard to other passages that nuance the meaning of the text. We should note also that the preference for a limited choice of passages is not unique to fundamentalism. Most Christians have favorite passages they go back to time and again. All denominations have certain passages that are key to their self-identity. Catholics have traditionally defended the papacy, the sacraments, and the hierarchical structure of the Church by means of certain passages in the Bible. The danger of this position is prooftexting, that is, seeking to justify one's argument by specific Bible passages that "prove" one's point. Creating a canon within the canon is always a risky move, for it ignores other passages that could inform one of God's will from an entirely different perspective. That is why the Catholic principle of reading the Bible within the context of the whole canon, not just a part of it, and in the larger context of church teaching, is helpful to maintaining a more objective approach to Scripture.

(5) A related deficiency to the one above is an ironic tendency to *equalize the authority of all parts of the Bible*. Just because the Bible says something, fundamentalists think it must have an application in the contemporary world. Yet this is precisely what makes it difficult for fundamentalists to deal with contradictions in the biblical text. There is no room for growth in the tradition or for development of a moral perspective that, in fact, changed over the many centuries that the Bible came into being. It is one thing to quote "an eye for an eye, and a tooth for a tooth" (Exod 21:24; Lev 24:19-20) as a principle for just punishment; it is another to quote Jesus' abrogation of this law (Matt 5:39). Both are in the Bible, but they surely have different meanings and different values. Also, minor issues are elevated to the level of serious teachings without much thought to a hierarchy of teachings (e.g., Paul's teaching about head coverings for women, 1 Cor 11:10). Not everything in the Bible has the same value.

(6) Another limitation of fundamentalism is its *failure to appreciate the incarnational dimension of faith*. I am not referring to the doctrine of the incarnation, the teaching that Jesus is God made man, but to the incarnational aspects of Christian faith that require a balance between the divine and the human. Fundamentalists ignore the ramifications that the Bible is God's Word *in human words*. Though the Bible contains God's message, human words express that message, and human words have limitations that require careful discernment. That is why interpreters must give careful attention to literary forms, vocabulary, sentence structure, and the like. The same lack of incarnational perspective affects the way fundamentalists view Jesus Christ. They often overemphasize the divine aspect to the detriment of his humanity.

Once when I was teaching a class on christology (the study of Jesus as the Christ, the messiah) to a small audience at which some fundamentalists were present, a question arose about Jesus' knowledge. Specifically, someone asked whether Jesus could read or write. I explained that the biblical evidence suggested that he could probably read (see Luke 4:16-20), at least Hebrew and Aramaic and probably some Koine Greek, the common language of the time. One of the fundamentalists strongly objected. He said, since Jesus was God, he naturally knew all languages! When I tried to explain my position on the basis of the biblical evidence, he simply could not abide by it and departed. He had so collapsed Jesus' divine nature into the human one that he held to what essentially was an ancient heresy, monophysitism—the belief only in Jesus' divine nature. Mainline Christian faith takes seriously the incarnational side of revelation, in relation both to Jesus Christ and to the Bible. Christian doctrine requires maintaining the tension between one aspect of a truth and another. It embraces a series of "both/and" propositions rather than "either/or" ones.

(7) Fundamentalism's *sidelining or outright rejection of the role of the Church* is another serious limitation. The overemphasis on personal faith, to the detriment of the communal aspects of faith, denigrates the role of the Church in a way that violates the spirit of the Bible. If we only read the Letters of Paul or the Acts of the Apostles we can see the importance of "church" as the community of disciples. Granted that there are abuses of overly-institutionalized religion that have crept into organized churches, one cannot reject outrightly the importance of the church community.

During the Jubilee Year 2000 Pope John Paul II called on members of the Catholic Church to confess their sinfulness and the sinfulness of our ancestors over the ages. The Church's leaders and members have hardly been perfect. Interestingly, some Protestant denominations followed this lead and did likewise. The communal dimension of Christian faith is apparent in such gestures. The fundamentalist perspective, on the other hand, ignores this communal dimension of salvation and places too much emphasis on personal salvation.

(8) Finally, I point to fundamentalism's *lack of appreciation of mystery*. The tendency to want everything to be explained rationally or to have no room for questions or ambiguity seriously undermines fundamentalists' ability to live in the modern world. The Bible is not a "divining" answer book. It is not a crystal ball made of paper. It does not provide a solution to every question human beings might pose to it. There is a point where we must acknowledge the limitations of our human knowledge and rely on the grace of God. In the end, we must acknowledge at times that God's intentions remain a mystery, and we will have to await further revelation of that mystery to unfold. In their desire for certainty, fundamentalists tend to ignore mystery in order to seek the rational, organized explanation of every facet of Christian faith. No room can be left for "fudging." This approach places mystery in a rather neat tidy package that can be easily explained and digested. In essence this weakness is an epistemological one. Epistemology is a fancy word for the philosophy of knowledge. It is the study of what people can know and how people come to knowledge of themselves and their world. Fundamentalists believe that they can know with absolute certainty God's will, especially as it is revealed in the Bible. But discerning God's will is not always as simple as the fundamentalist schema presumes.

The fundamentalist penchant for and fascination with apocalyptic expectation provides a case in point. Rather than spending endless hours speculating about the nature of events at the end of the world, for instance, most Christians simply acknowledge that we don't know. Some passages of the Bible itself support this direction. Paul warned some of his communities about the uselessness of speculating about the end time because it will come "like a thief in the night" (1 Thess 5:1-2). One of the sayings of Jesus reinforces this admonition by noting that only the Father knows the time line (Mark 13:32; Matt 24:36). We do not need to know every detail about how or when God's kingdom will come. To sustain Christian hope until Jesus comes in glory should suffice (1 Cor 11:26).

I have attempted to evaluate the pros and cons of fundamentalism fairly, but as a Roman Catholic, I obviously believe that the limitations of biblical fundamentalism seriously out-weigh its strong points. I also recognize that practical questions remain about how Catholics are to respond to the current fundamentalist challenge. We turn to this topic in our last chapter.

5

A Catholic Response to Fundamentalism

For many Catholics who encounter biblical fundamentalism in their daily lives, the main question is how to respond to it. I have been asked innumerable times, "Can you give me some answer to take back to my friend who says that Catholics aren't Bible-believing Christians?" Others have asked me for specific biblical passages to refute fundamentalists' accusations about Catholic practices, like addressing the priest as "father." In a sense, they want biblical ammunition to fight back.

Some authors have resurrected the time-honored tactic of apologetics (from Greek *apologia*, "defense speech") in an attempt to counter fundamentalist claims that Catholicism is not an authentic Christian faith (e.g., Karl Keating, *Catholicism and Fundamentalism* [San Francisco: Ignatius Press, 1988]; Scott and Kimberly Hahn, *Home Sweet Rome: Our Journey to Catholicism* [San Francisco: Ignatius Press, 1993]; and Philip St. Romain, *Respuestas Católicas a Preguntas Fundamentalistas* [Ligouri, Mo.: Ligouri Press, 1987]). Apologetics means defending the faith by offering rational explanations for the Church's position. A certain amount of apologetics is necessary in such situations, but I fear that it can be counterproductive. Apologetics presumes one can enter a dialogue with one's opponent.

In my experience dialogue is often not possible with fundamentalists. Conversation is more often one-sided, more a monologue than a dialogue. Those who believe they have the absolute, unalterable truth are not likely to find dialogue useful. (This goes for any position, not just fundamentalism.) Instead the conversation usually becomes a strong defense of one's own position, regardless of what is said by the conversation partner. More importantly, apologists for biblical interpretation can inadvertently fall into the same trap as their opponents, namely, misusing Scripture and relying as much on a literalistic interpretation of passages as their counterparts do. Nonetheless, I think there is a healthy Catholic response to fundamentalism that can be passed on to concerned Catholics. I boil them down to some do's and don'ts. Then, despite some misgivings, I will offer some apologetic advice on specific fundamentalist concerns that Catholics are likely to encounter.

The do's

(1) *DO educate yourself on the Bible.* The primary reason that Catholics are bothered by fundamentalist questions is that most of them are still uncomfortable with the contents of the Bible. Catholics are often intimidated by their Protestant friends or relatives who quote the Bible, chapter and verse, from memory. Despite the progress that has been made in Scripture education since the close of Vatican II, many Catholics have only a rudimentary knowledge of the Bible. St. Jerome made the famous observation, "Ignorance of the Scriptures is ignorance of Christ." We do encounter the risen Lord through the Bible, but I fear the results of more than thirty-five years of Catholic scholarship on the Bible have not been as far reaching as one would hope. Catholics need to reclaim the Bible as their own. Encouraging parish Bible study groups, Bible education sessions geared for all levels (children, teens, adults, seniors), and promoting individual study and prayer with the Bible should be a priority for Catholics.

The American bishops, in their brief pastoral letter on fundamentalism in the late 1980s, urged Catholic education on the Bible:

> We need a Pastoral Plan for the Word of God that will place
> the Sacred Scriptures at the heart of the parish and individual
> life. . . . In addition to that, we Catholics need to redouble
> our efforts to make our parish Masses an expression of wor-
> ship in which all–parishioners, visitors and strangers–feel the
> warmth and the welcome and know that here the Bible is
> clearly reverenced and preached. (*A Pastoral Statement for
> Catholics on Biblical Fundamentalism*, 7–8).

Although Catholic parishes have made progress in promoting the Word of God, I see no evidence of a unified pastoral
plan that has effectively heightened the general knowledge
of Catholics about the Bible. There are several good Bible
study programs available (Little Rock Scripture Study, Den-
ver Program, etc.) and many useful publications that give
good guidance for Catholics on the Bible (see Resources for
Further Study). Bible literacy should become a goal for Catholic parishes in the first decade of the new millennium. On a
personal level, Catholics should get into the habit of daily
Scripture readings and using the Bible for family prayer.
There is no substitute for direct familiarity with the Bible.

(2) *DO always read the Bible in context.* When reading
passages from the Bible always ask yourself what context it
is in. Context means a variety things. The most immediate
context of a passage is the surrounding material–what comes
before it, what comes after it. Then there is the context of
larger sections of the book (e.g., the chapters of a biblical
book) and the book of the Bible itself. Passages from Matthew are best understood in the context of that Gospel first,
before application is made to other sections of the New Testament. A third level of context is the historical one. Only
reference to a study Bible, commentary, footnotes, or outside
materials can provide this context, but it is crucial to understanding what the passage might have meant and in what
setting it emerged when it was written. Then there is the
larger context of the entire canon of Sacred Scripture. How
does the passage fit into the testimony of other Bible passages? Are there similar passages? Do other passages offer a
different perspective? Here again study aids are indispensable. Finally, one should ask how the passage fits into the

context of the Church's teaching. This last step acknowledges the limited perspective of each individual passage of the Bible in comparison to the overall testimony of faith through the ages. All this attention to context might sound complicated. It is not, once one gets the hang of it. But it is crucial to helping one understand properly how a specific Word of God applies in our own day by asking how it fits into the context into which it was born.

(3) *DO recognize the limitations of conversations with fundamentalists.* Catholics need to be realistic about what can be achieved by trying to converse with fundamentalists. At the outset, we have to acknowledge a huge chasm in our respective approaches to the Bible. They believe the Bible alone is a source of God's revelation. Catholics believe that Scripture and Tradition working in tandem with one another reveal God's will. Fundamentalists view the Bible's inerrancy or infallibility as absolute; Catholics accept the inerrancy of the Bible only in terms of faith and morals as taught in the Bible. These are presuppositions that cannot be bridged easily, if at all. We cannot expect to solve all our differences. On the other hand, we can capitalize on the elements we do have in common, such as the acceptance of faith in Jesus Christ, the power of the Bible to enliven Christian faith, the need to repent of sin and be forgiven, etc.

(4) *DO capitalize on the Catholic tradition.* In order for Catholics to address fundamentalist issues, they must be comfortable with their own Church's teaching about the Bible. Being secure in one's own faith is essential to being able to withstand a confrontation from another vantage point. My experience tells me that many Catholics are not only unfamiliar with the Bible itself but with the long and venerable teaching about the Bible in Catholic history. Fundamentalists do not view the Catholic faith as Bible-oriented, but as I have indicated earlier, that is a distortion of the reality. Catholicism is as committed to honoring and interpreting the Bible as God's Word as any other Christian denomination. In fact, Catholic teaching emphasizes that when the Scriptures are proclaimed, Christ is experienced as risen Lord (Vatican II's Constitution on the Sacred Liturgy, §7). Catho-

lic scholars may have come later than Protestant scholars to the well of God's Word, but when they arrived there they drank deeply. The average Catholic needs to become more familiar with official church teaching about the Bible, and parish priests, catechists, and educators need to make this more of a priority.

(5) *DO encourage good preaching from the Bible.* Roman Catholic seminaries today often promote excellent instruction in the Bible and in homiletics in ways that were not done in the days prior to Vatican Council II. Consequently, many priests and permanent deacons have received better instruction on the Bible and have been taught to preach the Word of God more effectively from the pulpit than ever before. The reality is, however, that among the ranks of fundamentalists are many disaffected Catholics who felt that they received little or no instruction from the clergy on the Bible. People should encourage their priests and deacons to proclaim the Word of God passionately and effectively. Good preaching resources abound today, and many dioceses have sponsored education days for their clergy that are geared to improve the quality of preaching. There is no foolproof method that makes a homily biblical, but the challenge to explain the Word of God in a non-technical way and apply it to people's lives accordingly is a task worthy of the clergy of every era.

(6) *DO promote a good community spirit in your parish.* Another reason that disaffected Catholics have fled to fundamentalist communities is that they feel more welcome, more at home, and a greater sense of belonging than they received in their parish. Large, impersonal Catholic parishes have to work hard at promoting such a community spirit. Many parishes have begun promoting small Christian faith communities to recapture some of that sense of community that is lost in a larger setting. Many have also instituted ministers of hospitality whose duty is to welcome people as they gather for worship, or host coffee and donut socials after Sunday Mass. Whatever method is used, Catholic parishes should be seen as welcoming communities. This advice applies to Sunday worship but also to the outreach efforts of parishes.

(7) *DO become comfortable with expressing your faith in personal terms.* Fundamentalists are unabashed in speaking about their faith. They wear it as a badge of honor. Many Catholics, on the other hand, find it difficult to speak of their faith in intensely personal or emotive terms. Catholicism has a more rational, systematic way of addressing faith that is less emotional. One of the post-conciliar renewal programs within the Catholic Church that was very appealing to some was the Catholic charismatic movement. Some fundamentalist groups are from the charismatic tradition. They emphasize the more emotional side of faith and the gifts of the Holy Spirit. The Catholic charismatic movement gave Catholics the freedom to express their faith in more personal and emotional terms. Not everyone needs literally to become a charismatic to be challenged to explore this more affective level of faith.

Another aspect of this issue is the need for Catholics to explore more the theme of evangelization. In preparation for the year 2000 and the new Christian millennium, Pope John Paul II strongly emphasized the need for Catholics to see evangelization as one of their important duties. Evangelization means the willingness to proclaim the gospel of Jesus Christ, in word and in deed, to all whom we encounter. It does not necessarily mean getting on one's soapbox and haranguing people. Evangelization means talking openly and comfortably about one's faith. It means disseminating Jesus' message clearly so that others may encounter it and embrace it. Since there are certainly disgruntled Catholics in the world, the message could well be directed to them first. In recent years many dioceses held large gatherings intended to reach out to those disaffected from the Catholic Church, often by means of large reconciliation services. The Pope's frank acknowledgments of the sins of Church members through two millennia of Christian history also added to this evangelical outreach. Acknowledging one's own failings and need for conversion is an excellent place to begin true evangelization, and it is part of the Catholic faith too. In fact, praying for one's own conversion should be uppermost in every Christian's mind before "doing battle" with the rest of the world.

The don'ts

While I can acknowledge some positive ways to address fundamentalism, I also point out some pitfalls:

(1) *DO NOT succumb to the temptation to make apologetics the answer.* The difficulty I find with a purely apologetic approach to fundamentalism is that it reduces everything to question and answer. Often it becomes a kind of "biblical jeopardy." Fundamentalists point out one passage of Scripture to defend a position, and Catholics counter with an opposite passage. As the story of Jesus' temptation points out, even the devil can quote Scripture (see Matt 4:1-11 and Luke 4:1-13). Because the Bible developed over a period of hundreds of years, there are inevitably contradictory passages in Scripture. Just about any passage in the Bible can be countered with an opposite message if one searches hard enough to find it. Playing a game of quotation-swapping solves little in the end. Apologetics can help to some degree, but at a certain point the fundamentalist and Catholic positions simply diverge. We will likely have to agree to disagree.

(2) *DO NOT make your interpretation THE interpretation.* A common mistake in interpreting the Bible is to assume that just because my interpretation makes sense to me, then that is what the passage must mean. We should avoid canonizing our own interpretation as *the* interpretation. We have to remain open to being enlightened by other alternative interpretations, some of which may be more informed than our own. Some might see in this advice an elitist agenda. I do not view it that way. Acknowledging that certain people are experts in biblical interpretation and have studied the field professionally, and therefore are likely to know much more than the average Christian who reads the Bible, is a fact that we ignore at our own peril.

(3) *DO NOT ridicule fundamentalism.* Making fun of one's opposition is never a good tactic. Catholics should not engage in stereotyping all fundamentalists nor should we promote unnecessarily an attitude of "we versus them." Some fundamentalists are bigoted anti-intellectuals, but some are not. While it is true that many radio and TV evangelists have

spoken some awful accusations against the Catholic Church, we should not respond likewise. This book has made it clear that fundamentalism is incompatible with Catholic faith, but I have endeavored to analyze the topic from a judicious and non-polemical vantage point.

Another reason to remain as objective as possible is that, if we are honest with ourselves, we will acknowledge that Catholics can fall into a type of fundamentalism as well. Some scholars have even gone so far as to assert the existence of a Catholic fundamentalism in which the magisterial teaching of the Church, narrowly understood, is used as a bludgeon to attack more liberal Catholics, all in the name of protecting orthodoxy. Perhaps it would best be termed "dogmatism" rather than fundamentalism. The fact is that an overly rigid and dogmatic approach to life can be found on both sides of the Catholic political spectrum, both the left and the right. In this sense, "fundamentalism" exists in many forms. Such people become self-proclaimed defenders of the faith, but they are not much different from diffident fundamentalists who hold to an a priori position without any thought of conversation. Furthermore, if fundamentalists have tended to flee to the Bible for prooftexts to uphold one doctrine or another, Catholics and other Christians have done the same. In other words, we should be mindful of our own limited approach to Scripture at times. As Jesus said, "Why do you see the speck in your neighbor's eye, but do not notice the log in your own eye?" (Matt 7:3). (The context in the Sermon on the Mount calls for Jesus' disciples to go beyond the usual approach to religion.) Everyone is called to recognize his or her own limitations and to heed the message of Jesus' call to conversion.

(4) *DO NOT take fundamentalism lightly*. Catholics need to be vigilant about the influence of fundamentalism. One survey recently suggested that some 30 percent of all Americans consider themselves "born again" Christians. We would be mistaken to dismiss fundamentalism as an irrelevant, outdated version of Christianity whose influence is small and insignificant. Surprising as it may seem, there have been recent legal battles over the teaching of the theory of evolu-

tion versus the teaching of creationism in public schools (e.g., in Kansas in 2000), on the basis of a fundamentalist reading of the book of Genesis. Fundamentalist evangelists on radio and TV still wield considerable influence among some sectors of the general population.

The "religious right," which includes fundamentalists, have made a concerted effort to influence the outcome of elections and to get their specific agenda addressed by changes in laws, in accordance with their democratic right. They are organized and well financed and feel it is their duty to re-shape the moral fabric of the United States. At times, what accompanies this fundamentalist perspective is a virulent form of anti-Catholicism, anti-Semitism, and anti-modern thought in general. In my estimation, Catholics should not ignore or underestimate the influence fundamentalism can wield in mainstream American life, even while we may agree with some of their political agenda (e.g., protecting the life of the unborn).

(5) *DO NOT give up hope.* In confrontations with fun-damentalists, we may be tempted to get dejected that the situation becomes a stalemate. Most frustrating for some Catholics is to see family members or close friends become entwined with a fundamentalist community. They become zealous for their new-found faith, and behavioral changes that affect the person can be difficult to tolerate, especially if they become pushy toward loved ones. Although I am skep-tical about the progress of dialogue between Catholics and fundamentalists, I remain ever hopeful that breakthroughs will one day occur. Unlike the Catholic Church and most mainline Protestant denominations which have embraced ecumenism, fundamentalists have not been quick to partici-pate in ecumenical and inter-faith dialogues. Catholics are viewed as the "enemy." In fact, when it concerns the ap-proach to the Bible, Catholics have more in common with mainline Protestant denominations than with fundamentalists. Nonetheless, I think we should sustain a hopeful stance and never give up trying to understand fundamentalists on their own terms, even when we choose to disagree with their stance.

How to respond to specific fundamentalist concerns

Above I warned about the limitations of apologetics in addressing biblical fundamentalism. Yet I am realistic in knowing that many Catholics seek some guidance on specific questions that they encounter from fundamentalist friends and relatives. To that end I offer the following advice on a few major questions that I think routinely crop up in encounters with fundamentalists. I emphasize that the best way to address these issues is to get further education on what the Bible does or does not teach.

Some frequently asked questions

• Why do Catholics believe in human traditions rather than the Bible?

What fundamentalists usually mean by "human traditions" is the collection of doctrines that form the basis of Catholic faith and that, to their mind, are not found in the Bible. A response to this query encompasses two issues. One is that contrary to fundamentalist perceptions, Catholics are indeed Bible-believing Christians. Catholics believe that the Bible is the Word of God, that it contains many essential teachings on faith and morality, and that it is absolutely vital for spiritual life. Since Vatican II, Catholics have also always celebrated all the sacraments with at least some form of reading from the Bible. Most important is the celebration of the Eucharist. At every Mass Catholics listen to excerpts from the Bible collected together into a book of readings called a "lectionary." On Sundays Catholics hear three readings and a psalm response; on weekdays there are two readings and a psalm response. One reading is always from one of the four canonical Gospels. Priests (or other homilists) are also expected to give at least a brief reflection on these readings to explain them and apply them to contemporary life. The Church also encourages Catholics to read, study, and pray the Bible on a regular basis.

The second response concerns the notion of "human traditions." Catholics do not believe that their Church's teachings are purely human in origin. Just as we accept the Holy Spirit's role in the inspiration of the Bible, so we believe the Holy Spirit guides the Church in its teaching and prevents it from falling into error in matters of doctrine and morality. We believe that the Holy Spirit guides the Church in formulating its doctrines that have evolved over time. That same Holy Spirit is the guarantor that the Church's teaching contains no errors in faith or morals. Fundamentalists mistakenly believe that their reliance upon the Bible is not based upon "human traditions," but that is not entirely true. As I noted earlier, a glance at the teachings contained in *The New Scofield Study Bible* shows that the explanations of Scripture contained in it are human interpretations that are not necessarily inherent in what the Bible says. So paradoxically many fundamentalist beliefs (such as the seven dispensations, the rapture, etc.) are human interpretations of the Bible rather than divine revelations.

• Where in the Bible does it say . . . ?

Many times people have asked me questions which began with this phrase. Generally they are seeking places where they can get a specific idea that will refute what a fundamentalist has claimed. I warned above that there is a danger in swapping Bible quotations. In the end that will not suffice. But sometimes Catholics just need assistance on how they might find a Bible passage that they may vaguely recall.

I will let you in on a little secret. Finding a specific passage in the Bible is actually not so difficult. All that it really takes is a Bible concordance. A concordance is a word list, tied to a specific version of the Bible, that sets forth all the passages where that word occurs. If one knows a major word of a biblical passage, all one must do is go to the list and look it up. This can be a tricky task, however. The concordance, usually available in a library if one does not own it, must be coordinated to a specific translation of the Bible. Of course, scholars use concordances of Greek and Hebrew for the original languages, but the principle is the same for English. There are various concordances available in retail bookstores that are geared to specific Bible translations.

Let's say one wants to know where in the Bible does it say you must "confess with your lips that Jesus Christ is Lord"? The main words one would look up are "confess" and "lips." Looking up a word like "Jesus" or "Lord" would take one to too many passages. The key is to make sure that the words one recalls are actually used in the translation. It so happens that the *New Revised Standard Version* does phrase a passage that way (Rom 10:9). The *New American Bible*, however, uses the phrase "if you confess with your mouth. . . ." You would find the passage by searching for the verb "confess" or the word "mouth" but not the noun "lips."

For those who are computerized, there is an even quicker method of finding passages. There are numerous Bible software programs on the market, some inexpensive and easy to use, that enable word searches and the like. If you really want to know where in the Bible something is said, get familiar with some form of a concordance.

- Why do Catholics use the title "father" for priests when the Bible forbids it?

Fundamentalists take Jesus' injunction in Matthew's Gospel literally about calling "no one father on earth, for you have one Father—the one in heaven" (23:9). They do not understand why Catholics would violate this passage by addressing priests as "father." First of all, one should note that the context of the Matthean passage concerns mistaken priorities and pride. Jesus preaches against people assuming titles and positions that place them above other people, whether it is rabbi, teacher, father, doctor, scholar, or any other title. The issue is not simply literally avoiding the title "father," but avoiding domination of others by reliance upon an external honor, position, or title that forgets one's true position of being servant of others.

With the specific term "father," Jesus is drawing a comparison made explicit frequently in Matthew's Gospel that God is the true Father of all. This is not a denial of earthly "fathers." Rather, Jesus calls his disciples to abandon all family relationships (Matt 4:22) and to enter a new family, the family of disciples (Matt 12:46-49), who together rely on the one Father who blesses and watches over them (see Matt 6:9). Jesus' injunction, then, is not to banish the title "father" from human vocabulary (either for biological fathers or for surrogate fathers), but to put it in its proper perspective vis-à-vis God's fatherhood. Not only that, but the New Testament demonstrates elsewhere that the image of father was not abandoned in the early Church. Paul, for instance, explicitly compared himself as a father in relation to his converts (1 Cor 4:15; Phil 2:22). Paul was not thereby rejecting Jesus' admonition. Instead, in 1 Corinthians 4:14-17 Paul uses the metaphor of a father and his "beloved children" to speak of both the love and the instruction which he imparts to them as his spiritual offspring (Greek *teknon*). He makes excellent use of the metaphor, going so far as to say explicitly, "in Christ Jesus I became your father through the gospel" (1 Cor 4:15).

Catholics thus use the term "father" for their priests out of respect for the office of priesthood and out of a desire to foster a true sense of the family of disciples whom Jesus gathered in his name. Priests are not to use their position for honor but for service to their sisters and brothers (Matt 20:26) whom they care for as a father does his children and a shepherd cares for his flock (Matt 9:36).

• Why do Catholics worship Mary and the saints?

Catholics do not *worship* Mary and the saints. Non-Catholics sometimes have the false impression that we do, but Catholics believe, along with all Christians, that only God deserves worship. We *honor* Mary and the saints because we believe they provide excellent role models for faith. Luke's Gospel, for example, portrays Mary in favorable terms that make of her a model disciple, for she is the one who perfectly hears and does the will of God. Her willingness to say "yes" to God's mysterious will offers the prime example of discipleship (Luke 1:26-38, 45; cf. 6:46-48). The Church continues to recognize saints and proclaim new ones in order to demonstrate that God's grace abounds across ethnic and national identities, extending to people from all walks of life, cultural heritage, and personal circumstances. Paintings and statues of such women and men of sanctity are used because they provide concrete images for people to reflect on. In no circumstance do Catholics worship such objects. They are mere aids to help visualize the model more explicitly.

- Why don't Catholics reject the theory of human evolution as contrary to the Bible?

Because Catholics do not believe the Bible to be inerrant in science or history, Catholics are not troubled by the modern scientific theory of evolution. We do not view it as contrary to the Bible at all. Nor do we view the Genesis account of creation as a literal explanation of how the universe came into being. So long as one believes that God ultimately lies behind creation and that creation is good, we find scientific explanations to be as plausible as the evidence that they can produce. In an address to the Pontifical Academy of Sciences (October 22, 1996), Pope John Paul II formally stated that the theory of evolution is not contrary to the Bible and does not contradict Catholic faith.

- Why do Catholics have a pope and bishops; they are not found in the Bible?

First, as pointed out in chapter three, Catholics do not accept that everything in our faith must stem from the Bible. So we must admit initially that we have totally different starting points.

On the issue of the hierarchical structure of the Church, Catholics believe that the papacy, the episcopacy, the priesthood, diaconate, and religious life have developed over time under the guidance of the Holy Spirit. We see these structures as rooted in the New Testament even while we acknowledge that the New Testament does not provide a blueprint for them. Catholics believe Jesus' words to Peter in Matthew's Gospel (16:16-19, "Blessed are you, Simon . . . You are Peter and upon this rock I will build my church . . .") form the basis of the Petrine ministry which became the papacy, a ministry of leadership and promoting unity. Other New Testament documents confirm Peter's special leadership role among the original twelve apostles as their spokesman. Ecumenical dialogues with some mainline Protestant communities have also led to their recognition of Peter's special role even if they do not necessarily accept the structure of the papacy.

Furthermore, some New Testament documents speak of presbyter-bishops who functioned as overseers and leaders of local churches. While these are not exact counterparts to present-day bishops, they form the background for the development of administrative offices that emerged when the Church grew more and more into an organization that needed formal shepherding. Later New Testament documents (e.g., 1–2 Timothy, Titus) show this increased institutionalization, leading to their designation as "the Catholic epistles." Once more, though, we must admit to fundamentalists that we do not believe contemporary church structures need to conform literally to specific biblical passages.

• Why do Catholics believe in the infallibility of the pope?

This question could seem curious, coming from fundamentalists who believe in the infallibility of the Bible. The point, of course, is to question how a human being could be infallible. We must point out that the Catholic teaching on papal infallibility, which was defined in the nineteenth century during Vatican Council I, applies only when the pope makes statements *ex cathedra* (Latin, literally meaning "from the seat" [of authority]; in ancient Jewish tradition one teaches authoritatively from a seated position), i.e., explicitly when pronouncing a formal dogmatic teaching. This has only been exercised twice in the history of the Church, to proclaim the doctrine of the Immaculate Conception of Mary (1854) and the doctrine of the Assumption of Mary (1950). Catholics believe that the Holy Spirit guides the Church in making such declarations, just as the Holy Spirit guided the authors of Scripture in communicating the truth in the areas of faith and morality. In each instance, God is the guarantor of truth. The humans are the vehicles through which the truth is communicated. Thus whether it is the infallibility of papal teaching that is at stake, or the religious truth of the Bible, divine authority is the source.

One caution to note is that many Catholics mistakenly think that just about any papal pronouncement that is made is infallible and must be believed. That is not the case. Catholics believe in a hierarchy of truths, some of which are central and others of which are more extraneous to the faith. Not every teaching has equal weight. Again, Catholics would acknowledge that the doctrine of infallibility is not in the Bible. We believe, however, that Jesus' promises to Peter which undergird the Petrine function of the papacy (Matt 16:16-19) function as a guarantee that God would never let the Church go astray in its proclamation of doctrines.

• Why do Catholics believe in the Church and the sacraments?

Contrary to many fundamentalists who view the Church with either indifference or outright contempt, Catholics believe the Church to be an essential part of God's plan of salvation. The Church is the people of God, the community of Jesus' disciples, called to bring Christ's message to the world by its life, its testimony, and its celebration of Word and sacraments. Many passages in the New Testament speak of the Church. Catholics particularly point to Matthew 16:16-18 as the key text for the Church's foundation, but many other texts speak of the functions of the Church (Acts 20:28; Eph 3:10; 1 Tim 3:15, etc.). Catholics also believe that the Old Testament itself foreshadowed the Church both in its explanation of the human race as a family God intended to be united in one community, and as an assembly of the chosen people, the people of Israel. In fact, the New Testament word for Church (Greek *ekklēsia*, "assembly, gathering, convocation" from the root *ekkalein*, "to be called out of") is rooted in a Old Testament notion of "assembly" (Hebrew *qahal*).

Catholics view the Church itself as a kind of "sacrament" (from Latin *sacramentum* "mystery, sign") which stands for the visible sign of the mystery of God's desire to unite people into one family. The seven sacraments (listed below) are external signs of God's invisible grace at work in the Church and in the world. Catholics believe each of these is rooted in the Bible but that their development in history has occurred under the guidance of the Holy Spirit. One must be careful, however, not to fall prey to the notion of prooftexting. Although Catholics believe the sacraments to be rooted in the Bible, we do not thereby think that everything the Church does, teaches, or believes about them must be found in Scripture. For reference to the biblical roots of the sacraments one can consult the following passages:

- baptism—John 3:5; Acts 2:38
- Eucharist—1 Cor 11:23-26; Matt 26:17-29; Mark 14:12-25; Luke 22:7-20
- confirmation—Acts 2:1-4
- reconciliation—John 20:22-23; 2 Cor 5:18
- matrimony—Gen 2:18-25; John 2:1-11
- holy orders—Mark 14:12-25 and parallels; 1 Tim 4:14; 2 Tim 1:6
- sacrament of the sick—James 5:14

- Why don't Catholics accept Jesus as their personal Lord and Savior?

Catholics do accept Jesus Christ as our personal Lord and Savior, but we do not approach this statement in the same fashion as fundamentalists. For fundamentalists, this is the quintessential statement of faith. They believe they must confess Jesus literally in word in order to be saved. They point to a passage in Romans to defend their stance (Rom 10:9). For Catholics, coming to faith and expressing it is a more complex and involved process. Catholics do not exaggerate the personal dimension of salvation. Jesus Christ came not simply to save me but the world. Salvation is mediated through a community of faith and not only through personal contact with Jesus. This is not to minimize the need for a personal commitment but to put it in its proper communal context.

- Why do Catholics baptize infants?

Nowhere does the Bible prohibit baptizing infants. Fundamentalists find difficulty with the Roman Catholic practice because of their emphasis on the personal decision that conversion to Christianity, according to their view, requires. Since infants cannot make such a conscious decision, baptizing them seems pointless. Catholics view conversion from a broader perspective. From the earliest days of the Church Christians baptized infants. The Bible hints at this, though it does not explicitly state it. In the Acts of the Apostles, for instance, conversion stories recount how "whole households" were baptized. Examples include Cornelius the Caesarean centurion and his household (Acts 10:47-48), Lydia the purple cloth dealer and her household (Acts 16:15), the Philippian jailer and "his entire family" (Acts 16:33), Crispus the Corinthian synagogue leader and his household (Acts 18:8), and Stephanas and his household (1 Cor 1:16; 16:15). To what does the word household (Greek *oikos*) refer? It includes husband, wife, children, and slaves, as well as free adults. Presumably it could have included infants, but that is never specifically attested.

More to the point is that Catholics do not view baptism as only an adult decision. Parents have their children baptized so that they can be raised in the faith that parents wish to pass on to their progeny. Naturally, at some point one's baptism must consciously be embraced (or confirmed) for authentic faith to mature. Catholics do not thereby ignore the need for a personal decision and commitment to one's faith.

• Why aren't Catholics "born again" Christians?

The inference of this question is usually the notion that Catholics aren't *really* Christians because they do not accept Jesus as their only personal Savior, do not consider themselves "born again," do not use the Bible, etc. Despite fundamentalists' accusations, Catholics are indeed Christians. A Christian is essentially anyone who follows Jesus Christ and his message. By virtue of our baptism and attempt to put into action Jesus' teachings, Catholics are no less Christian than anyone else who follows Jesus.

Of course, faith involves a lot more than a mere verbal assent. Fundamentalists have made the notion of being "born again" central to their faith. Catholics are not opposed to the idea of being born again. It is, after all, part of Jesus' teaching in the Gospel of John; yet one should note how infrequent such language is in the New Testament. We should examine the central passage a little more closely (John 3:3-6).

When Jesus tells the Jewish leader Nicodemus that he must be "born again" (Greek *anōthen*), he makes a play on words. The word can mean "from above" as well as "again." In John's world view, Jesus is the one who has come "from above" (the heavenly world), and he will return there, and eventually gather all his followers there. Jesus comes down to this world to point out its limitations and focus attention on the world above. Nicodemus misinterprets the saying to think he must crawl back into the womb. Thus, the notion of being born "again" is actually a misunderstanding. Jesus means that Nicodemus must be born anew, fresh, with the light of faith in Jesus. He goes on to tie in the notion with being born "of water and the Spirit," a clear allusion to baptism. Thus, being born "from above" includes being baptized and coming to faith in Jesus Christ. Curiously, most fundamentalists do not connect the notions of baptism and conversion, despite the biblical evidence that does so.

Catholics can accept the notion of being "born again" in the sense that faith requires ongoing conversion, over and over again, to Jesus Christ. It means making the spiritual life (the life above) the priority over earthly life (the life below). Although Catholics accept baptism as a one-time event, they do not believe that one's conversion can be reduced to a specific moment in time or place when we were "born again." Rather, we might say that we need to be born again and again and again. Catholics view conversion as an ongoing lifelong process. God's grace sometimes can dramatically act in a person's life for a sudden turnaround, but the normative experience is that most people experience a slow, gradual change in their lives as God's grace slowly works to transform them into better human beings. (For a more complete explanation of the New Testament teaching on conversion, see Ronald D. Witherup, *Conversion in the New Testament* [Collegeville: The Liturgical Press, 1994].)

• Why do Catholics believe they earn salvation through good works?

Catholics do not believe they earn salvation through their good works. At least, informed Catholics don't! This position has often been misunderstood. In the past, some of the Church's practices misled people into believing that they could somehow purchase salvation or earn it. This was one of Martin Luther's concerns in the sixteenth century when he called for Church reform. But authentic Catholic teaching acknowledges that salvation is a free gift from God achieved once and for all by the incarnation, suffering, death, and resurrection of Jesus Christ. No one earns salvation by doing good deeds. Instead, our good deeds demonstrate that we have put our faith into action.

For their part, fundamentalists overemphasize the biblical teaching of confessing Jesus as one's Savior to the detriment of other New Testament teachings. The Letter of James explicitly calls people to put their faith into action, for words without deeds are hollow (2:14-22). Catholics, for our part, should be careful not to give the impression to non-Catholics that we believe we can earn our place in heaven by what we say or do. That is the ancient heresy of Pelagianism, named for Pelagius, a fifth-century British monk who taught that humans could work toward salvation apart from divine grace. The Church found this approach wholly unacceptable and condemned Pelagius and his teaching.

• Why do Catholics confess their sins to a priest when only God can forgive sins?

Catholics do not confess their sins to the priest. They confess them to God. The priest is a vehicle, a mediator, who assists the penitent to come to terms with his or her sinfulness. It is God who forgives the sinner by the word of absolution pronounced by the priest. Catholics, too, believe that God alone forgives sin (though we are called to forgive one another, as expressed clearly in the Lord's Prayer), but we also believe that people can too often fool themselves if they do not have a concrete way of confronting their sinfulness.

Using a mediator to assist one with the process assures a more objective stance and lessens the possibility of glossing over our personal sinfulness. Catholics also point to the roots of the sacrament of reconciliation in the Bible (John 20:22-23, ". . . whose sins you shall forgive . . ."), but we acknowledge that the practice of private confession developed much later in church history, under the guidance of the Holy Spirit. For Catholics reconciliation is a sacrament, a visible sign of God's grace at work in the world forgiving sin.

• What do Catholics believe about the "rapture"?

Catholics do not accept the notion of the "rapture." The concept is not actually found in the Bible, though fundamentalists assert that it is. It is an interpretation of a passage in 1 Thessalonians in which Paul describes in vivid terms a scenario of the second coming of Christ (4:16-17). The word "rapture" (from Latin *rapere*, "seize, snatch") comes from Paul's expression that we will be "caught up" at the second coming of Christ when the dead are raised to new life in heaven. The fundamentalist doctrine emerged from *The Scofield Reference Bible* where it was first expounded. Later fundamentalist tracts have explained and expanded it. Often fundamentalists have invented very elaborate descriptions about how the events of the last days, the eschaton, will take place. The passage in Paul used to sustain the belief in the rapture is somewhat obscure and is in the larger context of Paul's teaching on the resurrection from the dead. It employs standard apocalyptic imagery (archangel's call, sound of the trumpet, the Lord coming on clouds) that is not meant to be a literal scenario of a step-by-step ascent to heaven. Paul's point is not to offer a preview of the process literally (though in his historical context he might have taken it so) but to assure the Thessalonians that the Lord was coming, and they would be taken up in glory.

While Catholics reject the idea of the rapture, they do hold to an expectation of the parousia (from Greek *parousia*, "coming"), the second coming of Christ. Catholics do not theorize about any particular time line or sequence of events, about when and how the eschaton will take place.

Instead, Catholics hold to a broad expectation that God will act definitively to establish the eternal kingdom in God's own good time and ways. In the meantime, Catholics believe in holding firm to their faith and remaining prepared in hopeful expectation of God's ultimate victory over evil.

Conclusion

These are certainly not the only questions that Catholics will likely meet when they are with their fundamentalist friends, but they are some of the ones encountered most frequently. I do not think naively that such responses would convince a fundamentalist to abandon his or her view and see the logic of the Catholic perspective. Recently, a participant at a workshop asked me why fundamentalists would not be convinced by my argumentation. The audience had raised many questions regarding fundamentalist objections to the Catholic faith, and I formulated responses to these. He said that he found the argumentation to be quite logical and convincing. But one person's logic is not always transparent to others. Fundamentalists are very zealous people. They have firm convictions formulated over time and consciously chosen. Argumentation alone, regardless of how rationally and peacefully it is presented, does not always win converts. That is why I do not ultimately have faith in apologetics alone. The best one can hope for is that a like-minded zeal rooted in a firm faith, sustained by a solid approach to biblical teaching, and rationally defended will give witness to fundamentalists that Catholics are conscientious Christians, too.

For the adventuresome reader who would like to explore more of these issues, the bibliographical list that follows will provide a good starting point to explore more deeply the phenomenon of fundamentalism and what Catholics can do to confront it. The first and foremost task, however, is to befriend the Bible. As the Spirit spoke long ago to St. Augustine the words that led to his conversion, "Tolle lege"–take up the sacred writings and read them. They will transform your life.

Resources for Further Study

On fundamentalism

Barr, James. *Beyond Fundamentalism*. Philadelphia: Westminster, 1984.

_____. *Fundamentalism*. Philadelphia: Westminster, 1978.

Boone, Kathleen C. *The Bible Tells Them So: The Discourse of Protestant Fundamentalism*. Albany, N.Y.: State University of New York Press, 1989.

Brown, Raymond E. "Biblical Fundamentalism: How Should Catholics Respond?" *St. Anthony Messenger* 98 (1990) 11–15.

_____. *Responses to 101 Questions on the Bible*. New York/Mahwah, N.J.: Paulist, 1990 (especially pp. 43–48, 137–42).

Cohen, Norman J. (ed.). *The Fundamentalist Phenomenon*. Grand Rapids, Mich.: Eerdmans, 1990.

Falwell, Jerry (ed.), with Ed Dobson and Ed Hindson. *The Fundamentalist Phenomenon: The Resurgence of Conservative Christianity*. 2nd. ed. Garden City, N.Y.: Doubleday, 1986.

Gilles, Anthony E. *Fundamentalism: What Every Catholic Needs to Know*. Cincinnati: St. Anthony Messenger, 1984.

Hoppe, Leslie J. "Premillennial Dispensationalism: Fundamentalism's Eschatological Scenario." *Chicago Studies* 34/3 (1995) 222–35.

LaVerdiere, Eugene. *Fundamentalism: A Pastoral Concern.* Collegeville: The Liturgical Press, 2000.

Marsden, George M. *Fundamentalism and American Culture: The Shaping of Twentieth Century Evangelicalism 1870–1925.* New York: Oxford University, 1980.

_____ (ed.). *Fundamentalism and Evangelicalism. Modern American Protestantism and Its World,* vol. 10. Munich/New York: K. G. Saur, 1993.

_____. *Understanding Fundamentalism and Evangelicalism.* Grand Rapids, Mich.: Eerdmans 1991.

Marty, Martin E. "Fundamentals of Fundamentalism." In *Fundamentalism in Comparative Perspective.* Lawrence Kaplan (ed.). Amherst, Mass: University of Massachusetts, 1992, 15–23.

Marty, Martin E., and R. Scott Appleby. *The Fundamentalisms Project.* 5 vols. Chicago: University of Chicago.
   vol. 1: *Fundamentalisms Observed.* 1991.
   vol. 2: *Fundamentalisms and Society: Reclaiming the Sciences, the Family, and Education.* 1993.
   vol. 3: *Fundamentalisms and the State: Remaking Politics, Economics, and Militance.* 1993.
   vol. 4: *Accounting for Fundamentalisms: The Dynamic Character of Movements.* 1994.
   vol. 5: *Fundamentalisms Comprehended.* 1995.

New Theology Review 1:2 (1988); entire issue devoted to fundamentalism.

O'Meara, Thomas F. *Fundamentalism: A Catholic Persspective.* New York/Mahwah, N.J.: Paulist, 1990.

A Pastoral Statement for Catholics on Biblical Fundamentalism. Washington, D.C.: NCCB/USCC, 1987 (English and Spanish).

Pontifical Biblical Commission. *The Interpretation of the Bible in the Church.* Boston: St. Paul Books & Media, 1993.

Witherup, Ronald D. *A Catholic Response to Biblical Fundamentalism.* Audio tape. Cincinnati: St. Anthony Messenger, 2000.

_____. "Catholicism and Fundamentalism." *The Bible Today* 32/1 (1994) 46–50.

_____. "Overview to *The Interpretation of the Bible in the Church.*" *The Bible Documents.* Chicago: Liturgy Training Publications, 2001, 122–28.

_____. "Is There a Catholic Approach to the Bible?" *The Priest* 51/2 (1995) 29–35.

_____. "The Use and Abuse of the Bible," *Scripture from Scratch* NO899. Cincinnati: St. Anthony Messenger, 1999.

_____. "Wrestling with the Rapture." *Chicago Studies* 34/3 (1995) 251–61.

On general Bible study

Bergant, Dianne, et al. (eds.). *The Collegeville Bible Commentary.* Collegeville: The Liturgical Press, 1989.

Brown, Raymond E. *Biblical Exegesis & Church Doctrine.* New York/Mahwah, N.J.: Paulist, 1985.

_____. *The Critical Meaning of the Bible.* New York/Ramsey: Paulist, 1981.

Brown, Raymond E., Joseph A. Fitzmyer, and Roland E. Murphy (eds.). *The New Jerome Biblical Commentary.* Englewood Cliffs, N.J.: Prentice-Hall, 1990 (especially articles ##19, 65, 66, and 72).

Coogan, Michael D., et al. (eds.). *The New Oxford Annotated Bible.* 3rd ed. New York: Oxford University Press, 2001.

Kee, Howard C., et al. *The Cambridge Companion to the Bible.* New York: Cambridge University Press, 1997.

Meeks, Wayne A., et al. (eds.). *The HarperCollins Study Bible.* New York: HarperCollins, 1993.

Senior, Donald, et al. (eds.). *The Catholic Study Bible.* New York: Oxford University Press, 1990.

Witherup, Ronald D. *The Bible Companion.* New York: Crossroad, 1998.

Suggestions for subscriptions

The Bible Today. A popular journal published six times a year and devoted to popularizing modern study of the Bible among Catholics. Available by subscription at $26 per year from The Liturgical Press, P.O. Box 7500, Collegeville, MN 56321-9989.

Scripture from Scratch. Monthly four-page pamphlets which explore timely biblical topics. Available in bulk as well as individual subscriptions. Individual price is $11 per year from St. Anthony Messenger Press, 1615 Republic Street, Cincinnati, OH 45210.